studysync®

Reading & Writing Companion

The Human Connection

studysync®

studysync.com

Send all inquiries to:
BookheadEd Learning, LLC
610 Daniel Young Drive
Sonoma, CA 95476

4 5 6 7 8 9 QSX 21 20 19 18 B

Cover, ©iStock.com/Rawpixel, ©iStock.com/DredK, ©iStock.com/alexey_boldin, ©iStock.com/skegbydave

STUDENT GUIDE

GETTING STARTED

Welcome to the StudySync Reading and Writing Companion! In this booklet, you will find a collection of readings based on the theme of the unit you are studying. As you work through the readings, you will be asked to answer questions and perform a variety of tasks designed to help you closely analyze and understand each text selection. Read on for an explanation of each section of this booklet.

CORE ELA TEXTS

In each Core ELA Unit you will read texts and text excerpts that share a common theme, despite their different genres, time periods, and authors. Each reading encourages a closer look with questions and a short writing assignment.

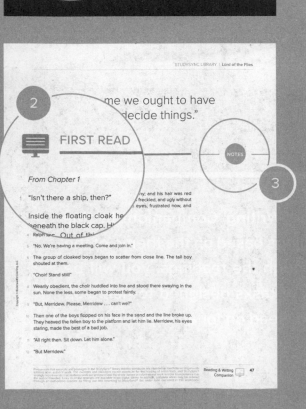

1 INTRODUCTION

An Introduction to each text provides historical context for your reading as well as information about the author. You will also learn about the genre of the excerpt and the year in which it was written.

2 FIRST READ

During your first reading of each excerpt, you should just try to get a general idea of the content and message of the reading. Don't worry if there are parts you don't understand or words that are unfamiliar to you. You'll have an opportunity later to dive deeper into the text.

3 NOTES

Many times, while working through the activities after each text, you will be asked to **annotate** or **make annotations** about what you are reading. This means that you should highlight or underline words in the text and use the "Notes" column to make comments or jot down any questions you may have. You may also want to note any unfamiliar vocabulary words here.

Reading & Writing Companion

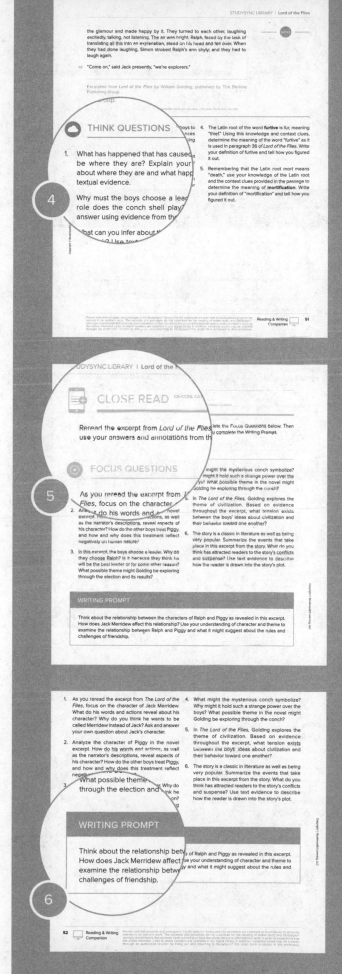

4 THINK QUESTIONS

These questions will ask you to start thinking critically about the text, asking specific questions about its purpose, and making connections to your prior knowledge and reading experiences. To answer these questions, you should go back to the text and draw upon specific evidence that you find there to support your responses. You will also begin to explore some of the more challenging vocabulary words used in the excerpt.

5 CLOSE READ & FOCUS QUESTIONS

After you have completed the First Read, you will then be asked to go back and read the excerpt more closely and critically. Before you begin your Close Read, you should read through the Focus Questions to get an idea of the concepts you will want to focus on during your second reading. You should work through the Focus Questions by making annotations, highlighting important concepts, and writing notes or questions in the "Notes" column. Depending on instructions from your teacher, you may need to respond online or use a separate piece of paper to start expanding on your thoughts and ideas.

6 WRITING PROMPT

Your study of each excerpt or selection will end with a writing assignment. To complete this assignment, you should use your notes, annotations, and answers to both the Think and Focus Questions. Be sure to read the prompt carefully and address each part of it in your writing assignment.

ENGLISH LANGUAGE DEVELOPMENT TEXTS

The English Language Development texts and activities take a closer look at the language choices that authors make to communicate their ideas. Individual and group activities will help develop your understanding of each text.

1 REREAD

After you have completed the First Read, you will have two additional opportunities to revisit portions of the excerpt more closely. The directions for each reread will specify which paragraphs or sections you should focus on.

2 USING LANGUAGE

These questions will ask you to analyze the author's use of language and conventions in the text. You may be asked to write in sentence frames, fill in a chart, or you may simply choose between multiple-choice options. To answer these questions, you should read the exercise carefully and go back in the text as necessary to accurately complete the activity.

3 MEANINGFUL INTERACTIONS & SELF-ASSESSMENT RUBRIC

After each reading, you will participate in a group activity or discussion with your peers. You may be provided speaking frames to guide your discussions or writing frames to support your group work. To complete these activities, you should revisit the excerpt for textual evidence and support. When you finish, use the Self-Assessment Rubric to evaluate how well you participated and collaborated.

EXTENDED WRITING PROJECT

The Extended Writing Project is your opportunity to explore the theme of each unit in a longer written work. You will draw information from your readings, research, and own life experiences to complete the assignment.

1 WRITING PROJECT

After you have read all of the unit text selections, you will move on to a writing project. Each project will guide you through the process of writing an argumentative, narrative, informative, or literary analysis essay. Student models and graphic organizers will provide guidance and help you organize your thoughts as you plan and write your essay. Throughout the project, you will also study and work on specific writing skills to help you develop different portions of your writing.

2 WRITING PROCESS STEPS

There are five steps in the writing process: **Prewrite, Plan, Draft, Revise,** and **Edit, Proofread, and Publish.** During each step, you will form and shape your writing project so that you can effectively express your ideas. Lessons focus on one step at a time, and you will have the chance to receive feedback from your peers and teacher.

3 WRITING SKILLS

Each Writing Skill lesson focuses on a specific strategy or technique that you will use during your writing project. The lessons begin by analyzing a student model or mentor text, and give you a chance to learn and practice the skill on its own. Then, you will have the opportunity to apply each new skill to improve the writing in your own project.

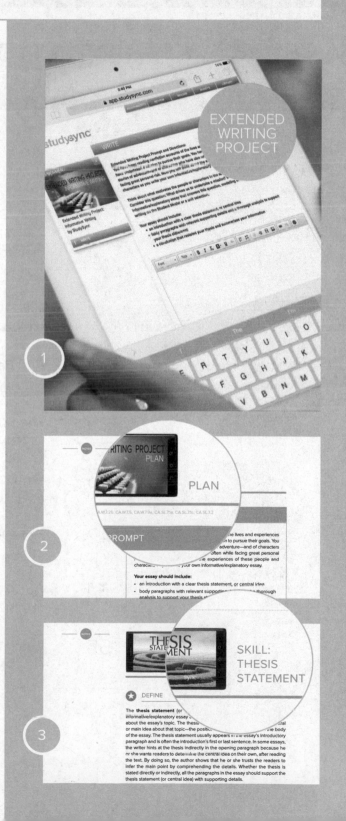

The Human Connection

TEXTS

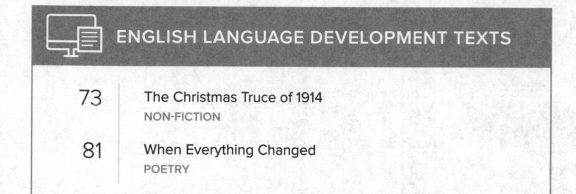

ENGLISH LANGUAGE DEVELOPMENT TEXTS

EXTENDED WRITING PROJECT

130

Text Fulfillment
through
StudySync

PLUTARCH'S LIVES

NON-FICTION
Plutarch
1579

INTRODUCTION

Plutarch, an ancient Greek historian, biographer, and essayist, is most famous for his series of parallel biographies about Greek and Roman leaders, known as *Plutarch's Lives*. Plutarch explored the qualities of each leader in order to establish a link between their character and political destiny. In the 16th century, Sir Thomas North translated Plutarch's work into English, and it was North's translation that Shakespeare consulted when writing several of his historical plays, including *Julius Caesar*. The excerpts here come from three different chapters in *Plutarch's Lives*, but all describe the same event—the riot that erupted at Caesar's funeral.

"Brutus committed two great faults..."

 FIRST READ

NOTES

From Volume 7: Caesar

Caesar's funerals

1   The next morning, Brutus and his confederates came into the market-place to speak unto the people, who gave them such audience, that it seemed they neither greatly **reproved,** nor allowed the fact: for by their great silence they shewed, that they were sorry for Caesar's death, and also that they did reverence Brutus. Now the Senate granted general pardon for all that was past, and to pacify every man, ordained besides, that Caesar's funerals should be honoured as a god, and established all things that he had done: and gave certain provinces also, and convenient honours unto Brutus and his confederates, whereby every man thought all things were brought to good peace and quietness again. But when they had opened Caesar's testament, and found a liberal legacy of money, bequeathed unto every citizen of Rome, and that they saw his body (which was brought into the market-place) all bemangled with gashes of swords: then there was no order to keep the multitude and common people quiet, but they plucked up forms, tables, and stools, and laid them all about the body, and setting them afire, burnt the corpse. Then when the fire was well kindled, they took the firebrands, and went unto their houses that had slain Caesar, to set them afire.

From Volume 9: Brutus

Brutus committed two great faults

2   Then Antonius thinking good [Caesar's] testament should be read openly, and also that his body should be honourably buried, and not in hugger-mugger, lest the people might thereby take occasion to be worse offended if they did otherwise: Cassius stoutly spake against it. But Brutus went with the

motion, and agreed unto it: wherein it seemeth he committed a second fault. For the first fault he did was, when he would not consent to his fellow-conspirators, that Antonius should be slain. And therefore he was justly accused, that thereby he had saved and strengthened a strong and grievous enemy of their conspiracy. The second fault was, when he agreed that Caesar's funerals should be as Antonius would have them: the which indeed **marred** all. For first of all, when Caesar's testament was openly read among them, whereby it appeared that he bequeathed unto every citizen of Rome, seventy-five drachmas a man, and that he left his gardens and arbours unto the people, which he had on this side of the river of Tiber, in the place where now the temple of Fortune is built: the people then loved him, and were marvellous sorry for him. Afterwards when Caesar's body was brought into the market-place, Antonius making his funeral oration in praise of the dead, according to the ancient custom of Rome, and perceiving that his words moved the common people to compassion: he framed his **eloquence** to make their hearts yearn the more, and taking Caesar's gown all bloody in his hand, he laid it open to the sight of them all, shewing what a number of cuts and holes it had upon it. Therewithal the people fell presently into such a rage and mutiny, that there was no more order kept amongst the common people.

From Volume 9: Antonius

Antonius maketh uproar among the people

3 But now, the opinion he conceived of himself after he had a little felt the goodwill of the people towards him, hoping thereby to make himself the chiefest man if he might overcome Brutus: did easily make him alter his first mind. And therefore when Caesar's body was brought to the place where it should be buried, he made a funeral oration in **commendation** of Caesar, according to the ancient custom of praising noblemen at their funerals. When he saw that the people were very glad and desirous also to hear Caesar spoken of, and his praises uttered: he mingled his orations with lamentable words, and by amplifying of matters did greatly move their hearts and affections unto pity and compassion. In fine to conclude his oration, he unfolded before the whole assembly the bloody garments of the dead, thrust through in many places with their swords, and called the **malefactors,** cruel and cursed murtherers. With these words he put the people into such a fury, that they presently took Caesar's body, and burnt it in the market-place, with such tables and forms as they could get together. Then when the fire was kindled, they took firebrands, and ran to the murtherer's houses to set them on fire, and to make them come out to fight.

Copyright © BookheadEd Learning, LLC

☁ THINK QUESTIONS CA-CCSS: CA.RI.9-10.1, CA.RI.9-10.4, CA.L.9-10.4a, CA.L.9-10.4d, CA.L.9-10.4b

1. According to the biography of Caesar, how did the people's attitude toward him change during his funeral and why?

2. In the excerpt from the biography of Brutus, what made the people fall "into such a rage and mutiny"? Use evidence from the text to support your response.

3. What does the excerpt from Antonius's biography suggest about his motivation for speaking at Caesar's funeral and thus reveal about his character? Use evidence from the text to support your response.

4. Use context to determine the meaning of the word **malefactors** as it is used in the text. Write your definition of "malefactors" here and describe how you arrived at it. Then look up "malefactors" in a dictionary and compare the dictionary definition with your own.

5. Recall that the Latin suffix "-*ation*" forms a noun from a verb form. Based on this knowledge, provide a definition of the word **commendation** as it is used in the text, and explain how you arrived at it.

Please note that excerpts and passages in the StudySync® library and this workbook are intended as touchstones to generate interest in an author's work. The excerpts and passages do not substitute for the reading of entire texts, and StudySync® strongly recommends that students seek out and purchase the whole literary or informational work in order to experience it as the author intended. Links to online resellers are available in our digital library. In addition, complete works may be ordered through an authorized reseller by filling out and returning to StudySync® the order form enclosed in this workbook.

Reading & Writing Companion **7**

CLOSE READ

CA-CCSS: CA.RI.9-10.1, CA.RI.9-10.2, CA.RI.9-10.6, CA.W.9-10.2a, CA.W.9-10.2b, CA.W.9-10.4, CA.W.9-10.5, CA.W.9-10.6, CA.W.9-10.9b, CA.W.9-10.10

Reread the excerpt from *Plutarch's Lives*. As you reread, complete the Focus Questions below. Then use your answers and annotations from the questions to help you complete the Writing Prompt.

FOCUS QUESTIONS

1. What is the central or main idea of the excerpt from Caesar's biography, entitled "Caesar's funerals"? Write a summary of the paragraph.

2. According to Plutarch, what two "faults" does Brutus commit? What do you think Brutus's interactions with his co-conspirators suggest about his character?

3. What is the central or main idea of the excerpt from Antonius's biography? How effectively does the title express the main idea of the passage?

4. Analyze the persuasive tactics Antonius uses during his funeral oration, as described by Plutarch.

5. What do Antonius's interactions with the crowd suggest about his character?

WRITING PROMPT

What do Plutarch's descriptions of the people and events in this part of Roman history reveal about his own point of view or attitude toward them? Identify and analyze the central ideas that emerge from Plutarch's descriptions of Caesar, Brutus, and Antonius, what these reveal about how Plutarch perceives their characters, and what links he draws between their qualities as leaders and their political destinies. Cite evidence from the text to support your response.

Reading & Writing Companion

JULIUS CAESAR

DRAMA
William Shakespeare
1599

INTRODUCTION

Shakespeare's *Julius Caesar* was modeled on historic events in Rome, 44 B.C, with the central characters based on members of the Senate, where infighting and power struggles were the order of the day. Believing that Caesar had acquired too much power, Cassius and Brutus led a successful campaign to assassinate him on March 15, the infamous Ides of March. Shakespeare re-enacts these events and the dramatic consequences that follow while exploring the conflict between loyalty and nationalism. In this passage, Brutus and Antony offer alternate interpretations of Caesar's murder in order to sway the plebeians.

"Friends, Romans, countrymen, lend me your ears..."

 FIRST READ

Excerpt from ACT III SCENE II. The Forum.

1 *[Enter Brutus and Cassius, with a throng of Citizens.]*

2 CITIZENS.
3 We will be satisfied; let us be satisfied.

4 BRUTUS.
5 Then follow me, and give me audience, friends.—
6 Cassius, go you into the other street
7 And part the numbers.—
8 Those that will hear me speak, let 'em stay here;
9 Those that will follow Cassius, go with him;
10 And public reasons shall be **rendered**
11 Of Caesar's death.

12 FIRST CITIZEN.
13 I will hear Brutus speak.

14 SECOND CITIZEN.
15 I will hear Cassius; and compare their reasons,
16 When severally we hear them rendered.

17 *[Exit Cassius, with some of the Citizens. Brutus goes into the rostrum.]*

18 THIRD CITIZEN.
19 The noble Brutus is ascended: silence!

20 BRUTUS.
21 Be patient till the last.
22 Romans, countrymen, and lovers! Hear me for my cause; and be
23 silent, that you may hear: believe me for mine honour, and have

NOTES

24 respect to mine honor, that you may believe: **censure** me in your
25 wisdom; and awake your senses, that you may the better judge.
26 If there be any in this assembly, any dear friend of Caesar's, to
27 him I say that Brutus' love to Caesar was no less than his. If
28 then that friend demand why Brutus rose against Caesar, this is
29 my answer,—Not that I loved Caesar less, but that I loved Rome
30 more. Had you rather Caesar were living, and die all slaves, than
31 that Caesar were dead, to live all freemen? As Caesar loved me, I
32 weep for him; as he was fortunate, I rejoice at it; as he was
33 valiant, I honour him; but, as he was ambitious, I slew him.
34 There is tears for his love; joy for his fortune; honour for his
35 valour; and death for his ambition. Who is here so base that
36 would be a bondman? If any, speak; for him have I offended. Who
37 is here so rude that would not be a Roman? If any, speak; for him
38 have I offended. Who is here so vile that will not love his
39 country? If any, speak; for him have I offended. I pause for a
40 reply.

41 CITIZENS.
42 None, Brutus, none.

43 BRUTUS.
44 Then none have I offended. I have done no more to Caesar
45 than you shall do to Brutus. The question of his death is
46 enroll'd in the Capitol, his glory not **extenuated,** wherein he
47 was worthy; nor his offenses enforced, for which he suffered
48 death.

49 *[Enter Antony and others, with Caesar's body.]*

50 Here comes his body, mourned by Mark Antony, who, though he had
51 no hand in his death, shall receive the benefit of his dying, a
52 place in the commonwealth; as which of you shall not? With this
53 I depart— that, as I slew my best lover for the good of Rome, I
54 have the same dagger for myself, when it shall please my country
55 to need my death.

56 CITIZENS.
57 Live, Brutus! live, live!

58 FIRST CITIZEN.
59 Bring him with triumph home unto his house.

60 SECOND CITIZEN.
61 Give him a statue with his ancestors.

Copyright © Bookheaded Learning, LLC

62 THIRD CITIZEN.
63 Let him be Caesar.

64 FOURTH CITIZEN.
65 Caesar's better parts
66 Shall be crown'd in Brutus.

67 FIRST CITIZEN.
68 We'll bring him to his house with shouts and clamours.

69 BRUTUS.
70 My countrymen,—

71 SECOND CITIZEN.
72 Peace! silence! Brutus speaks.

73 FIRST CITIZEN.
74 Peace, ho!

75 BRUTUS.
76 Good countrymen, let me depart alone,
77 And, for my sake, stay here with Antony:
78 Do grace to Caesar's corpse, and grace his speech
79 Tending to Caesar's glory; which Mark Antony,
80 By our permission, is allow'd to make.
81 I do entreat you, not a man depart,
82 Save I alone, till Antony have spoke.

83 *[Exit.]*

84 FIRST CITIZEN.
85 Stay, ho! and let us hear Mark Antony.

86 THIRD CITIZEN.
87 Let him go up into the public chair;
88 We'll hear him.—Noble Antony, go up.

89 ANTONY.
90 For Brutus' sake, I am beholding to you.

91 *[Goes up.]*

92 FOURTH CITIZEN.
93 What does he say of Brutus?

NOTES

94 THIRD CITIZEN.
95 He says, for Brutus' sake,
96 He finds himself beholding to us all.

97 FOURTH CITIZEN.
98 'Twere best he speak no harm of Brutus here.

99 FIRST CITIZEN.
100 This Caesar was a tyrant.

101 THIRD CITIZEN.
102 Nay, that's certain:
103 We are blest that Rome is rid of him.

104 SECOND CITIZEN.
105 Peace! let us hear what Antony can say.

106 ANTONY.
107 You gentle Romans,—

108 CITIZENS.
109 Peace, ho! let us hear him.

110 ANTONY.
111 Friends, Romans, countrymen, lend me your ears;
112 I come to bury Caesar, not to praise him.
113 The evil that men do lives after them;
114 The good is oft interred with their bones:
115 So let it be with Caesar. The noble Brutus
116 Hath told you Caesar was ambitious:
117 If it were so, it was a grievous fault;
118 And grievously hath Caesar answer'd it.
119 Here, under leave of Brutus and the rest,—
120 For Brutus is an honourable man;
121 So are they all, all honorable men,—
122 Come I to speak in Caesar's funeral.
123 He was my friend, faithful and just to me:
124 But Brutus says he was ambitious;
125 And Brutus is an honourable man.
126 He hath brought many captives home to Rome,
127 Whose ransoms did the general **coffers** fill:
128 Did this in Caesar seem ambitious?
129 When that the poor have cried, Caesar hath wept:
130 Ambition should be made of sterner stuff:
131 Yet Brutus says he was ambitious;
132 And Brutus is an honourable man.

Please note that excerpts and passages in the StudySync® library and this workbook are intended as touchstones to generate interest in an author's work. The excerpts and passages do not substitute for the reading of entire texts, and StudySync® strongly recommends that students seek out and purchase the whole literary or informational work in order to experience it as the author intended. Links to online resellers are available in our digital library. In addition, complete works may be ordered through an authorized reseller by filling out and returning to StudySync® the order form enclosed in this workbook.

 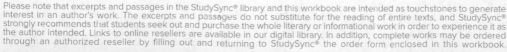

133 You all did see that on the Lupercal
134 I thrice presented him a kingly crown,
135 Which he did thrice refuse: was this ambition?
136 Yet Brutus says he was ambitious;
137 And, sure, he is an honourable man.
138 I speak not to disprove what Brutus spoke,
139 But here I am to speak what I do know.
140 You all did love him once,—not without cause:
141 What cause withholds you, then, to mourn for him?—
142 O judgment, thou art fled to brutish beasts,
143 And men have lost their reason!—Bear with me;
144 My heart is in the coffin there with Caesar,
145 And I must pause till it come back to me.

146 FIRST CITIZEN.
147 Methinks there is much reason in his sayings.

148 SECOND CITIZEN.
149 If thou consider rightly of the matter,
150 Caesar has had great wrong.

151 THIRD CITIZEN.
152 Has he not, masters?
153 I fear there will a worse come in his place.

154 FOURTH CITIZEN.
155 Mark'd ye his words? He would not take the crown;
156 Therefore 'tis certain he was not ambitious.

157 FIRST CITIZEN.
158 If it be found so, some will dear abide it.

159 SECOND CITIZEN.
160 Poor soul! his eyes are red as fire with weeping.

161 THIRD CITIZEN.
162 There's not a nobler man in Rome than Antony.

163 FOURTH CITIZEN.
164 Now mark him; he begins again to speak.

165 ANTONY.
166 But yesterday the word of Caesar might
167 Have stood against the world: now lies he there,
168 And none so poor to do him reverence.
169 O masters, if I were disposed to stir

170 Your hearts and minds to mutiny and rage,

171 I should do Brutus wrong and Cassius wrong,

172 Who, you all know, are honourable men:

173 I will not do them wrong; I rather choose

174 To wrong the dead, to wrong myself, and you,

175 Than I will wrong such honourable men.

176 But here's a parchment with the seal of Caesar,—

177 I found it in his closet,—'tis his will:

178 Let but the commons hear this testament,—

179 Which, pardon me, I do not mean to read,—

180 And they would go and kiss dead Caesar's wounds,

181 And dip their napkins in his sacred blood;

182 Yea, beg a hair of him for memory,

183 And, dying, mention it within their wills,

184 **Bequeathing** it as a rich legacy

185 Unto their issue.

186 FOURTH CITIZEN.

187 We'll hear the will: read it, Mark Antony.

188 CITIZENS.

189 The will, the will! We will hear Caesar's will.

190 ANTONY.

191 Have patience, gentle friends, I must not read it;

192 It is not meet you know how Caesar loved you.

193 You are not wood, you are not stones, but men;

194 And, being men, hearing the will of Caesar,

195 It will inflame you, it will make you mad.

196 'Tis good you know not that you are his heirs;

197 For if you should, O, what would come of it!

198 FOURTH CITIZEN.

199 Read the will! we'll hear it, Antony;

200 You shall read us the will,—Caesar's will!

201 ANTONY.

202 Will you be patient? will you stay awhile?

203 I have o'ershot myself to tell you of it:

204 I fear I wrong the honorable men

205 Whose daggers have stabb'd Caesar; I do fear it.

206 FOURTH CITIZEN.

207 They were traitors: honourable men!

208 CITIZENS.
209 The will! The testament!

210 SECOND CITIZEN.
211 They were villains, murderers. The will! read the will!

212 ANTONY.
213 You will compel me, then, to read the will?
214 Then make a ring about the corpse of Caesar,
215 And let me show you him that made the will.
216 Shall I descend? and will you give me leave?

217 CITIZENS.
218 Come down.

219 SECOND CITIZEN.
220 Descend.

221 *[He comes down.]*

222 THIRD CITIZEN.
223 You shall have leave.

224 FOURTH CITIZEN.
225 A ring! stand round.

226 FIRST CITIZEN.
227 Stand from the hearse, stand from the body.

228 SECOND CITIZEN.
229 Room for Antony!—most noble Antony!

230 ANTONY.
231 Nay, press not so upon me; stand far' off.

232 CITIZENS.
233 Stand back; room! bear back.

234 ANTONY.
235 If you have tears, prepare to shed them now.
236 You all do know this mantle: I remember
237 The first time ever Caesar put it on;
238 'Twas on a Summer's evening, in his tent,
239 That day he overcame the Nervii.
240 Look, in this place ran Cassius' dagger through:
241 See what a rent the envious Casca made:

NOTES

242 Through this the well-beloved Brutus stabb'd;
243 And as he pluck'd his cursed steel away,
244 Mark how the blood of Caesar follow'd it,—
245 As rushing out of doors, to be resolved
246 If Brutus so unkindly knock'd, or no;
247 For Brutus, as you know, was Caesar's angel:
248 Judge, O you gods, how dearly Caesar loved him!
249 This was the most unkindest cut of all;
250 For when the noble Caesar saw him stab,
251 Ingratitude, more strong than traitors' arms,
252 Quite vanquish'd him: then burst his mighty heart;
253 And, in his mantle muffling up his face,
254 Even at the base of Pompey's statua,
255 Which all the while ran blood, great Caesar fell.
256 O, what a fall was there, my countrymen!
257 Then I, and you, and all of us fell down,
258 Whilst bloody treason flourish'd over us.
259 O, now you weep; and, I perceive, you feel
260 The dint of pity: these are gracious drops.
261 Kind souls, what, weep you when you but behold
262 Our Caesar's vesture wounded? Look you here,
263 Here is himself, marr'd, as you see, with traitors.

264 FIRST CITIZEN.
265 O piteous spectacle!

266 SECOND CITIZEN.
267 O noble Caesar!

268 THIRD CITIZEN.
269 O woeful day!

270 FOURTH CITIZEN.
271 O traitors, villains!

272 FIRST CITIZEN.
273 O most bloody sight!

274 SECOND CITIZEN.
275 We will be revenged.

276 CITIZENS.
277 Revenge,—about,—seek,—burn,—fire,—kill,—slay,—let not a
278 traitor live!

279 ANTONY.
280 Stay, countrymen.

281 FIRST CITIZEN.
282 Peace there! hear the noble Antony.

283 SECOND CITIZEN.
284 We'll hear him, we'll follow him, we'll die with him.

285 ANTONY.
286 Good friends, sweet friends, let me not stir you up
287 To such a sudden flood of mutiny.
288 They that have done this deed are honourable:
289 What private griefs they have, alas, I know not,
290 That made them do it; they're wise and honourable,
291 And will, no doubt, with reasons answer you.
292 I come not, friends, to steal away your hearts:
293 I am no orator, as Brutus is;
294 But, as you know me all, a plain blunt man,
295 That love my friend; and that they know full well
296 That gave me public leave to speak of him:
297 For I have neither wit, nor words, nor worth,
298 Action, nor utterance, nor the power of speech,
299 To stir men's blood: I only speak right on;
300 I tell you that which you yourselves do know;
301 Show you sweet Caesar's wounds, poor dumb mouths,
302 And bid them speak for me: but were I Brutus,
303 And Brutus Antony, there were an Antony
304 Would ruffle up your spirits, and put a tongue
305 In every wound of Caesar, that should move
306 The stones of Rome to rise and mutiny.

307 CITIZENS.
308 We'll mutiny.

309 FIRST CITIZEN.
310 We'll burn the house of Brutus.

311 THIRD CITIZEN.
312 Away, then! come, seek the conspirators.

313 ANTONY.
314 Yet hear me, countrymen; yet hear me speak.

315 CITIZENS.
316 Peace, ho! hear Antony; most noble Antony!

NOTES

317 ANTONY.
318 Why, friends, you go to do you know not what.
319 Wherein hath Caesar thus deserved your loves?
320 Alas, you know not; I must tell you then:
321 You have forgot the will I told you of.

322 CITIZENS.
323 Most true; the will!—let's stay, and hear the will.

324 ANTONY.
325 Here is the will, and under Caesar's seal.
326 To every Roman citizen he gives,
327 To every several man, seventy-five drachmas.

328 SECOND CITIZEN.
329 Most noble Caesar!—we'll revenge his death.

330 THIRD CITIZEN.
331 O, royal Caesar!

332 ANTONY.
333 Hear me with patience.

334 CITIZENS.
335 Peace, ho!

336 ANTONY.
337 Moreover, he hath left you all his walks,
338 His private arbors, and new-planted orchards,
339 On this side Tiber: he hath left them you,
340 And to your heirs forever; common pleasures,
341 To walk abroad, and recreate yourselves.
342 Here was a Caesar! when comes such another?

343 FIRST CITIZEN.
344 Never, never.—Come, away, away!
345 We'll burn his body in the holy place,
346 And with the brands fire the traitors' houses.
347 Take up the body.

348 SECOND CITIZEN.
349 Go, fetch fire.

350 THIRD CITIZEN.
351 Pluck down benches.

Please note that excerpts and passages in the StudySync® library and this workbook are intended as touchstones to generate interest in an author's work. The excerpts and passages do not substitute for the reading of entire texts, and StudySync® strongly recommends that students seek out and purchase the whole literary or informational work in order to experience it as the author intended. Links to online resellers are available in our digital library. In addition, complete works may be ordered through an authorized reseller by filling out and returning to StudySync® the order form enclosed in this workbook.

Reading & Writing Companion   19

NOTES

352 FOURTH CITIZEN.
353 Pluck down forms, windows, any thing.

354 *[Exeunt Citizens, with the body.]*

355 ANTONY.
356 Now let it work.—Mischief, thou art afoot,
357 Take thou what course thou wilt!—

THINK QUESTIONS CA-CCSS: CA.RL.9-10.1, CA.RL.9-10.4, CA.L.9-10.4a

1. Use details from the text to support your understanding of why, according to Brutus, he and other senators killed Caesar. Provide evidence that is directly stated in the selection as well as ideas that you have inferred from clues in the text.

2. Write a few sentences explaining why Mark Antony refers to Brutus and the other conspirators as "honourable" men. What examples of Caesar's ambition does Mark Antony raise and why? Cite evidence from the text to support your answers.

3. How does Mark Antony use Caesar's will to sway the emotions of the citizens? Support your answer with evidence from the text.

4. Use context to determine the meaning of the word **rendered** as it is used in *Julius Caesar*. Write your definition of "rendered" here and tell how you found it. Then use a dictionary to confirm this meaning.

5. Use context to determine the meaning of the word **coffers** as it is used in *Julius Caesar*. Write your definition of "coffers" here and tell how you found it.

CLOSE READ

CA-CCSS: CA.RL.9-10.1, CA.RL.9-10.3, CA.RL.9-10.7, CA.RL.9-10.9, CA.W.9-10.1a, CA.W.9-10.1b, CA.W.9-10.4, CA.W.9-10.5, CA.W.9-10.6, CA.W.9-10.9a, CA.W.9-10.10

Reread the excerpt from *Julius Caesar.* As you reread, complete the Focus Questions below. Then use your answers and annotations from the questions to help you complete the Writing Prompt.

FOCUS QUESTIONS

1. Explain how Shakespeare uses Brutus's opening speech to set the scene. Then analyze the persuasive tactics Brutus uses in this speech and to what effect. What does Brutus mean when he says after it, "Then none have I offended"?

2. Reread Brutus's final words to the crowd before he leaves the Forum. Why do you think Brutus requests that "not a man depart" until Mark Antony has spoken of Caesar? How might the film clip of these lines from the 2012 Royal Shakespeare Company stage production shed light on this question?

3. Compare and contrast Plutarch's treatment of Antony's remarks about Caesar's garments with Shakespeare's treatment of the same. What was Antony's motivation for this display?

4. Compare and contrast the role of the crowd in Plutarch's text with the role it plays in Shakespeare's play. Why are the crowds important? In what ways are the two crowds alike and different?

5. Compare and contrast the characters of Brutus and Antony as they are revealed in Act III, Scene II, of *Julius Caesar*. How are they most alike and most different? How do their actions and interactions define them?

WRITING PROMPT

How does Shakespeare transform the source material from Sir Thomas North's translation of *Plutarch's Lives* in Act III, Scene II of his play *Julius Caesar*? In what ways are the two texts similar and different? Use your understanding of comparison and contrast to explore how and why Shakespeare incorporated, expanded upon, and deviated from Plutarch's accounts of Caesar's funeral in the biographies of Caesar, Brutus, and Antonius. How did such transformations enhance the development of character and theme in the play? What dramatic effects might these artistic decisions on Shakespeare's part have been intended to have on the audience, and how have different film versions illustrated these effects in different ways? Support your writing with evidence from the text.

Please note that excerpts and passages in the StudySync® library and this workbook are intended as touchstones to generate interest in an author's work. The excerpts and passages do not substitute for the reading of entire texts, and StudySync® strongly recommends that students seek out and purchase the whole literary or informational work in order to experience it as the author intended. Links to online resellers are available in our digital library. In addition, complete works may be ordered through an authorized reseller by filling out and returning to StudySync® the order form enclosed in this workbook.

Reading & Writing Companion **21**

CIVIL PEACE

FICTION
Chinua Achebe
1972

INTRODUCTION

Chinua Achebe was a Nigerian novelist, poet, essayist and lecturer. Amid some controversy, Achebe elected to write in English, "the language of colonizers," in order to reach the broadest possible audience. He is best known for his novel *Things Fall Apart*, which remains today the most widely read work of African literature. In the short story here, "Civil Peace," Achebe provides a true-to-life description of Nigeria in the early 1970s, shortly after the Biafran War

"Nothing puzzles God."

FIRST READ

1   Jonathan Iwegbu counted himself extraordinarily lucky. "Happy survival!" meant so much more to him than just a current fashion of greeting old friends in the first hazy days of peace. It went deep to his heart. He had come out of the war with five inestimable blessings—his head, his wife Maria's head and the heads of three out of their four children. As a bonus he also had his old bicycle—a miracle too but naturally not to be compared to the safety of five human heads.

2   The bicycle had a little history of its own. One day at the height of the war it was commandeered "for urgent military action." Hard as its loss would have been to him he would still have let it go without a thought had he not had some doubts about the genuineness of the officer. It wasn't his disreputable rags, nor the toes peeping out of one blue and one brown canvas shoes, nor yet the two stars of his rank done obviously in a hurry in biro, that troubled Jonathan; many good and heroic soldiers looked the same or worse. It was rather a certain lack of grip and firmness in his manner. So Jonathan, suspecting he might be **amenable** to influence, rummaged in his raffia bag and produced the two pounds with which he had been going to buy firewood which his wife, Maria, retailed to camp officials for extra stock-fish and corn meal, and got his bicycle back. That night he buried it in the little clearing in the bush where the dead of the camp, including his own youngest son, were buried. When he dug it up again a year later after the surrender all it needed was a little palm-oil greasing. "Nothing puzzles God," he said in wonder.

3   He put it to immediate use as a taxi and accumulated a small pile of Biafran money ferrying camp officials and their families across the four-mile stretch to the nearest tarred road. His standard charge per trip was six pounds and those who had the money were only glad to be rid of some of it in this way. At the end of a fortnight he had made a small fortune of one hundred and fifteen pounds.

4   Then he made the journey to Enugu and found another miracle waiting for him. It was unbelievable. He rubbed his eyes and looked again and it was still

standing there before him. But, needless to say, even that monumental blessing must be accounted also totally inferior to the five heads in the family. This newest miracle was his little house in Ogui Overside. Indeed nothing puzzles God! Only two houses away a huge concrete edifice some wealthy contractor had put up just before the war was a mountain of rubble. And here was Jonathan's little zinc house of no regrets built with mud blocks quite intact! Of course the doors and windows were missing and five sheets off the roof. But what was that? And anyhow he had returned to Enugu early enough to pick up bits of old zinc and wood and soggy sheets of cardboard lying around the neighbourhood before thousands more came out of their forest holes looking for the same things. He got a **destitute** carpenter with one old hammer, a blunt plane and a few bent and rusty nails in his tool bag to turn this assortment of wood, paper and metal into door and window shutters for five Nigerian shillings or fifty Biafran pounds. He paid the pounds, and moved in with his overjoyed family carrying five heads on their shoulders.

5   His children picked mangoes near the military cemetery and sold them to soldiers' wives for a few pennies—real pennies this time—and his wife started making breakfast akara balls for neighbours in a hurry to start life again. With his family earnings he took his bicycle to the villages around and bought fresh palm-wine which he mixed generously in his rooms with the water which had recently started running again in the public tap down the road, and opened up a bar for soldiers and other lucky people with good money.

6   At first he went daily, then every other day and finally once a week, to the offices of the Coal Corporation where he used to be a miner, to find out what was what. The only thing he did find out in the end was that the little house of his was even a greater blessing than he had thought. Some of his fellow ex-miners who had nowhere to return at the end of the day's waiting just slept outside the doors of the offices and cooked what meal they could **scrounge** together in Bournvita tins. As the weeks lengthened and still nobody could say what was what Jonathan discontinued his weekly visits altogether and faced his palm-wine bar.

7   But nothing puzzles God. Came the day of the windfall when after five days of endless scuffles in queues and counter-queues in the sun outside the Treasury he had twenty pounds counted into his palms as ex-gratia award for the rebel money he had turned in. It was like Christmas for him and for many others like him when the payments began. They called it (since few could manage its proper official name) egg-rasher.

8   As soon as the pound notes were placed in his palm Jonathan simply closed it tight over them and buried fist and money inside his trouser pocket. He had to be extra careful because he had seen a man a couple of days earlier collapse into near-madness in an instant before that oceanic crowd because no sooner had he got his twenty pounds than some heartless **ruffian** picked

it off him. Though it was not right that a man in such an extremity of agony should be blamed yet many in the queues that day were able to remark quietly on the victim's carelessness, especially after he pulled out the innards of his pocket and revealed a hole in it big enough to pass a thief's head. But of course he had insisted that the money had been in the other pocket, pulling it out too to show its comparative wholeness. So one had to be careful.

9   Jonathan soon transferred the money to his left hand and pocket so as to leave his right free for shaking hands should the need arise, though by fixing his gaze at such an elevation as to miss all approaching human faces he made sure that the need did not arise, until he got home.

10   He was normally a heavy sleeper but that night he heard all the neighbourhood noises die down one after another. Even the night watchman who knocked the hour on some metal somewhere in the distance had fallen silent after knocking one o'clock. That must have been the last thought in Jonathan's mind before he was finally carried away himself. He couldn't have been gone for long, though, when he was violently awakened again.

11   'Who is knocking?' whispered his wife lying beside him on the floor.

12   "I don't know," he whispered back breathlessly.

13   The second time the knocking came it was so loud and imperious that the rickety old door could have fallen down.

14   "Who is knocking?" he asked then, his voice parched and trembling.

15   "Na tief-man and him people," came the cool reply. "Make you hopen de door." This was followed by the heaviest knocking of all.

16   Maria was the first to raise the alarm, then he followed and all their children.

17   *"Police-o! Thieves-o! Neighbours-o! Police-o! We are lost! We are dead! Neighbours, are you asleep? Wake up! Police-o!"*

18   This went on for a long time and then stopped suddenly. Perhaps they had scared the thief away. There was total silence. But only for a short while.

19   "You done finish?" asked the voice outside. "Make we help you small. Oya, everybody!"

20   *"Police-o! Tief-man-o! Neighbours-o! we done loss-o! Police-o!. . ."*

21   There were at least five other voices besides the leader's.

22   Jonathan and his family were now completely paralysed by terror. Maria and the children sobbed inaudibly like lost souls. Jonathan groaned continuously.

23　The silence that followed the thieves' alarm vibrated horribly. Jonathan all but begged their leader to speak again and be done with it.

24　"My frien," said he at long last, "we don try our best for call dem but I tink say dem all done sleep-o. . . So wetin we go do now? Sometaim you wan call soja? Or you wan make we call dem for you? Soja better pass police. No be so?"

25　"Na so!" replied his men. Jonathan thought he heard even more voices now than before and groaned heavily. His legs were sagging under him and his throat felt like sand-paper.

26　"My frien, why you no de talk again. I de ask you say you wan make we call soja?"

27　"No."

28　"Awrighto. Now make we talk business. We no be bad tief. We no like for make trouble. Trouble done finish. War done finish and all the katakata wey de for inside. No Civil War again. This time na Civil Peace. No be so?"

29　"Na so!" answered the horrible chorus.

30　'What do you want from me? I am a poor man. Everything I had went with this war. Why do you come to me? You know people who have money. We. . .'

31　"Awright! We know say you no get plenty money. But we sef no get even anini. So derefore make you open dis window and give us one hundred pound and we go commot. Orderwise we de come for inside now to show you guitar-boy like dis. . ."

32　A volley of automatic fire rang through the sky. Maria and the children began to weep aloud again.

33　"Ah, missisi de cry again. No need for dat. We done talk say we na good tief. We just take our small money and go nwayorly. No molest. Abi we de molest?"

34　"At all!" sang the chorus.

35　"My friends," began Jonathan hoarsely. "I hear what you say and I thank you. If I had one hundred pounds. . ."

36　"Lookia my frien, no be play we come play for your house. If we make mistake and step for inside you no go like am-o. So derefore. . ."

37　"To God who made me; if you come inside and find one hundred pounds, take it and shoot me and shoot my wife and children. I swear to God. The only money I have in this life is this twenty-pounds egg-rasher they gave me today. . ."

38 "OK. Time de go. Make you open dis window and bring the twenty pound. We go manage am like dat."

39 There were now loud murmurs of dissent among the chorus: 'Na lie de man de lie; e get plenty money. . . Make we go inside and search properly well... Wetin be twenty pound?. . .

40 "Shurrup!" rang the leader's voice like a lone shot in the sky and silenced the murmuring at once. "Are you dere? Bring the money quick!"

41 "I am coming," said Jonathan fumbling in the darkness with the key of the small wooden box he kept by his side on the mat.

42 At the first sign of light as neighbours and others assembled to **commiserate** with him he was already strapping his five-gallon demijohn to his bicycle carrier and his wife, sweating in the open fire, was turning over akara balls in a wide clay bowl of boiling oil. In the corner his eldest son was rinsing out dregs of yesterday's palm wine from old beer bottles.

43 "I count it as nothing," he told his sympathizers, his eyes on the rope he was tying. "What is egg-rasher? Did I depend on it last week? Or is it greater than other things that went with the war? I say, let egg-rasher perish in the flames! Let it go where everything else has gone. Nothing puzzles God."

 THINK QUESTIONS CA-CCSS: CA.RL.9-10.1, CA.RL.9-10.4, CA.L.9-10.4a, CA.L.9-10.4b

1. How did the civil war affect Jonathan and his neighbors? How does Jonathan begin to rebuild his life after the war? Cite textual evidence to support your answer.

2. What is Jonathan like as a person? Support your answer with textual evidence.

3. How do Jonathan's neighbors respond when he calls for help? Make an inference about why, and support it with evidence.

4. Use context to determine the meaning of the word **scrounge** as it is used in *Civil Peace*. Write your definition of "scrounge" here and tell how you found it.

5. Remembering that the Latin prefix *com-* means "together with" and the Latin suffix *-ate* indicates an action, and comparing **commiserate** to the familiar words "miserable" and "misery," use the context clues provided in the passage to determine the meaning of "commiserate." Write your definition of "commiserate" here and tell how you got it.

Please note that excerpts and passages in the StudySync® library and this workbook are intended as touchstones to generate interest in an author's work. The excerpts and passages do not substitute for the reading of entire texts, and StudySync® strongly recommends that students seek out and purchase the whole literary or informational work in order to experience it as the author intended. Links to online resellers are available in our digital library. In addition, complete works may be ordered through an authorized reseller by filling out and returning to StudySync® the order form enclosed in this workbook.

Reading & Writing Companion   **27**

CLOSE READ
CA-CCSS: CA.RL.9-10.1, CA.RL.9-10.2, CA.RL.9-10.3, CA.RL.9-10.6, CA.W.9-10.1a, CA.W.9-10.1b, CA.W.9-10.2, CA.W.9-10.4, CA.W.9-10.5, CA.W.9-10.6, CA.W.9-10.9a, CA.W.9-10.10

Reread the short story "Civil Peace." As you reread, complete the Focus Questions below. Then use your answers and annotations from the questions to help you complete the Writing Prompt.

FOCUS QUESTIONS

1. In the first two paragraphs of "Civil Peace," Jonathan's bicycle is one of the main topics. Why is the bicycle so important in setting up the story? What is the author conveying about the cultural context by focusing on the bicycle? Highlight evidence from the text and make annotations to support your interpretation.

2. Returning to the city of Enugu, Jonathan and his family begin a new life. What do their activities tell you about the cultural context? Support your answer with textual evidence and make annotations to explain your answer.

3. In the eighth paragraph, Jonathan thinks about the incident of the man who was robbed of his *ex gratia* award. He also thinks about the response of onlookers to the robbery. State two inferences that you make about the cultural context based on that incident. Highlight your textual evidence and make annotations to support your inferences.

4. The last third of the story describes Jonathan's encounter with the robbers. What is the leader of the robbers like? How do his interactions with Jonathan help define who he is? Highlight and annotate evidence from the text to support your analysis.

5. In the concluding two paragraphs, Jonathan's neighbors commiserate with him, and he explains his feelings to them. What theme do his words convey? Highlight textual evidence and make annotations to support your point.

WRITING PROMPT

What theme is conveyed by the story's repeated statement, "Nothing puzzles God"? What does the statement reveal about Jonathan's character? What does it show about the cultural context of Jonathan's life? Write a response to these questions. Cite evidence from the story to support your response.

THE BOOK THIEF

FICTION
Markus Zusak
2005

INTRODUCTION

Australian author Markus Zusak's acclaimed novel is set in Nazi Germany, where foster child Liesel Meminger develops an unusual passion—stealing books. Narrated by Death, who describes how busy he was at the time, the story focuses on Liesel's love for books as well as her relationships with her parents, her neighbors, and a Jewish fighter hiding in her basement. In the excerpt below, Death tells of his first encounter with the protagonist, then nine years old.

"It's the leftover humans. The survivors."

FIRST READ

Part 1: DEATH AND CHOCOLATE

1   First the colors.

2   Then the humans.

3   That's usually how I see things.

4   Or at least, how I try.

5   ***HERE IS A SMALL FACT ***
               You are going to die.

6   I am in all truthfulness attempting to be cheerful about this whole topic, though most people find themselves hindered in believing me, no matter my **protestations**. Please, trust me. I most definitely can be cheerful. I can be amiable. Agreeable. **Affable**. And that's only the A's. Just don't ask me to be nice. Nice has nothing to do with me.

7   ***Reaction to the ***
               AFOREMENTIONED fact
               Does this worry you? urge you
               —don't be afraid.
               I'm nothing if not fair.

8   —Of course, an introduction.

9   A beginning.

10 Where are my manners?

Copyright © BookheadEd Learning, LLC

11 I could introduce myself properly, but it's not really necessary. You will know me well enough and soon enough, depending on a diverse range of variables. It suffices to say that at some point in time, I will be standing over you, as genially as possible. Your soul will be in my arms. A color will be perched on my shoulder. I will carry you gently away.

12 At that moment, you will be lying there (I rarely find people standing up). You will be caked in your own body. There might be a discovery; a scream will dribble down the air. The only sound I'll hear after that will be my own breathing, and the sound of the smell, of my footsteps.

13 The question is, what color will everything be at that moment when I come for you? What will the sky be saying?

14 Personally, I like a chocolate-colored sky. Dark, dark chocolate. People say it suits me. I do, however, try to enjoy every color I see—the whole spectrum. A billion or so flavors, none of them quite the same, and a sky to slowly suck on. It takes the edge off the stress. It helps me relax.

15 ****** A SMALL THEORY ******
People observe the colors of a day only at its beginnings and ends, but to me it's quite clear that a day merges through a multitude of shades and intonations, with each passing moment. A single hour can consist of thousands of different colors. Waxy yellows, cloud-spat blues. Murky darknesses.
In my line of work, I make it a point to notice them.

16 As I've been alluding to, my one saving grace is distraction. It keeps me sane. It helps me cope, considering the length of time I've been performing this job. The trouble is, who could ever replace me? Who could step in while I take a break in your stock-standard resort-style vacation destination, whether it be tropical or of the ski trip variety? The answer, of course, is nobody, which has prompted me to make a conscious, deliberate decision—to make distraction my vacation. Needless to say, I vacation in **increments.** In colors.

17 Still, it's possible that you might be asking, why does he even need a vacation? What does he need distraction from?

18 Which brings me to my next point.

19 It's the leftover humans. The survivors.

20 They're the ones I can't stand to look at, although on many occasions I still fail. I deliberately seek out the colors to keep my mind off them, but now and then, I witness the ones who are left behind, crumbling among the jigsaw

Copyright © BookheadEd Learning, LLC

puzzle of realization, despair, and surprise. They have punctured hearts. They have beaten lungs.

21 Which in turn brings me to the subject I am telling you about tonight, or today, or whatever the hour and color. It's the story of one of those perpetual survivors—an expert at being left behind.

22 It's just a small story really, about, among other things:

23 › A girl
   › Some words
   › An accordionist
   › Some fanatical Germans* A Jewish fist fighter
   › And quite a lot of thievery

24 I saw the book thief three times.

Part 2: BESIDE THE RAILWAY LINE

25 First up is something white. Of the blinding kind.

26 Some of you are most likely thinking that white is not really a color and all of that tired sort of nonsense. Well, I'm here to tell you that it is. White is without question a color, and personally, I don't think you want to argue with me.

27 *****A REASSURING ANNOUNCEMENT *****
Please, be calm, despite that previous threat.
I am all bluster—
I am not violent.
I am not malicious.
I am a result.

28 Yes, it was white.

29 It felt as though the whole globe was dressed in snow. Like it had pulled it on, the way you pull on a sweater.

30 Next to the train line, footprints were sunken to their shins. Trees wore blankets of ice.

31 As you might expect, someone had died.

32 They couldn't just leave him on the ground. For now, it wasn't such a problem, but very soon, the track ahead would be cleared and the train would need to move on.

33 There were two guards.

NOTES

34 There was one mother and her daughter.

35 One corpse.

36 The mother, the girl, and the corpse remained stubborn and silent.

37 "Well, what else do you want me to do?"

38 The guards were tall and short. The tall one always spoke first, though he was not in charge. He looked at the smaller, rounder one. The one with the juicy red face.

39 "Well," was the response, "we can't just leave them like this, can we?"

40 The tall one was losing patience. "Why not?"

41 And the smaller one damn near exploded. He looked up at the tall one's chin and cried, "Spinnst du! Are you stupid?!" The abhorrence on his cheeks was growing thicker by the moment. His skin widened. "Come on," he said, traipsing over the snow. "We'll carry all three of them back on if we have to. We'll notify the next stop."

42 As for me, I had already made the most elementary of mistakes. I can't explain to you the severity of my self-disappointment. Originally, I'd done everything right:

43 I studied the blinding, white-snow sky who stood at the window of the moving train. I practically inhaled it, but still, I wavered. I buckled—I became interested. In the girl. Curiosity got the better of me, and I resigned myself to stay as long as my schedule allowed, and I watched.

44 Twenty-three minutes later, when the train was stopped, I climbed out with them.

45 A small soul was in my arms.

46 I stood a little to the right.

47 The dynamic train guard duo made their way back to the mother, the girl, and the small male corpse. I clearly remember that my breath was loud that day. I'm surprised the guards didn't notice me as they walked by. The world was sagging now, under the weight of all that snow.

48 Perhaps ten meters to my left, the pale, empty-stomached girl was standing, frost-stricken.

49 Her mouth jittered.

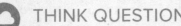

NOTES

50 Her cold arms were folded.

51 Tears were frozen to the book thief's face.

Excerpted from *The Book Thief* by Markus Zusak, published by Alfred A. Knopf.

THINK QUESTIONS   CA-CCSS: CA.RL.9-10.1, CA.L.9-10.4d, CA.L.9-10.4a

1. Which aspect of the world most fascinates the narrator of *The Book Thief*? Why? Cite details from the text to support your response.

2. How does Death react to the survivors after he takes a life? Why does he react this way? Cite details from the text in your response.

3. Based on your knowledge of what was taking place in Europe during the 1940s, why do you think the author chose Death to narrate this story? Provide reasons or evidence to explain your response.

4. Look up the definition of **protestation** in a dictionary. Then rewrite the sentence in which the word "protestations" appears in the selection, replacing this term with a synonym.

5. Use context to determine the meaning of the word **increments** as it is used within the text. Write your definition of "increments" here.

CLOSE READ

CA-CCSS: CA.RL.9-10.1, CA.RL.9-10.2, CA.RL.9-10.3, CA.RL.9-10.5, CA.W.9-10.2a, CA.W.9-10.2b, CA.W.9-10.4, CA.W.9-10.5, CA.W.9-10.6, CA.W.9-10.9a, CA.W.9-10.10

Reread the excerpt from *The Book Thief*. As you reread, complete the Focus Questions below. Then use your answers and annotations from the questions to help you complete the Writing Prompt.

FOCUS QUESTIONS

1. In the first part of the excerpt, why does the narrator value escape from his work and feel a need for occasional relief? How is this helpful to him? Support your answer with textual evidence and make annotations to explain your answer choices.

2. Analyze the format and writing style author Markus Zusak uses at the beginning of the second passage. How does the story structure affect readers? What does it help them understand? Highlight evidence from the text and make annotations to support your explanation.

3. In the second passage, how does the narrator describe the Book Thief? Which details does he include? What do these details help the reader to visualize? Highlight evidence from the text and make annotations to explain your choices.

4. What do readers learn about the Book Thief in the second passage? Who is she and where is she? What has happened to her recently? What might this foreshadow? Support your answer with textual evidence and make annotations to explain your answer choices.

5. How do Death's interactions with survivors affect him? How might his interactions with the Book Thief define and shape him as the story progresses? Highlight textual evidence and make annotations to explain your ideas.

WRITING PROMPT

How does the imagery of color work in this excerpt? Choose at least three instances of color imagery in this excerpt and analyze what it represents and how it adds to the meaning of the passage as a whole. Your analysis should be at least 300 words long and you should use quotes from the text in support of your assertions.

NIGHT

NON-FICTION
Elie Wiesel
1955

INTRODUCTION

studysync tv

Nobel Prize winner Elie Wiesel's autobiographical account of a Jewish teenager and his father struggling to stay alive in a World War II concentration camp delivers an impact that few readers can ever forget. The narrator describes his first night at Birkenau and its indelible physical and mental effects on him, then and since.

"Never shall I forget those flames that consumed my faith forever."

FIRST READ

From Section 3

1   Never shall I forget that night, the first night in camp, that turned my life into one long night seven times sealed.

2   Never shall I forget that smoke.

3   Never shall I forget the small faces of the children whose bodies I saw transformed into smoke under a silent sky.

4   Never shall I forget those flames that consumed my faith forever.

5   Never shall I forget the **nocturnal** silence that deprived me for all eternity of the desire to live.

6   Never shall I forget those moments that murdered my God and my soul and turned my dreams to ashes.

7   Never shall I forget those things, even were I condemned to live as long as God Himself.

8   Never.

9   The barrack we had been assigned to was very long. On the roof, a few bluish skylights. I thought: This is what the **antechamber** of hell must look like. So many crazed men, so much shouting, so much brutality.

10   Dozens of inmates were there to receive us, sticks in hand, striking anywhere, anyone, without reason. The orders came:

11   "Strip! Hurry up! *Raus!* Hold on only to your belt and your shoes . . ."

12 Our clothes were to be thrown on the floor at the back of the barrack. There was a pile there already. New suits, old ones, torn overcoats, rags. For us it meant true equality: nakedness. We trembled in the cold.

13 A few SS officers wandered through the room, looking for strong men. If vigor was that appreciated, perhaps one should try to appear sturdy? My father thought the opposite. Better not to draw attention. (We later found out that he had been right. Those who were selected that day were incorporated into the Sonder-Kommando, the Kommando working in the **crematoria.** Béla Katz, the son of an important merchant of my town, had arrived in Birkenau with the first transport, one week ahead of us. When he found out that we were there, he succeeded in slipping us a note. He told us that having been chosen because of his strength, he had been forced to place his own father's body into the furnace.)

14 The blows continued to rain on us:

15 "To the barber!"

16 Belt and shoes in hand, I let myself be dragged along to the barbers. Their clippers tore out our hair, shaved every hair on our bodies. My head was buzzing; the same thought surfacing over and over: not to be separated from my father.

17 Freed from the barbers' clutches, we began to wander about the crowd, finding friends, acquaintances. Every encounter filled us with joy—yes, joy: Thank God! You are still alive!

18 Some were crying. They used whatever strength they had left to cry. Why had they let themselves be brought here? Why didn't they die in their beds? Their words were **interspersed** with sobs.

19 Suddenly someone threw his arms around me in a hug: Yehiel, the Sigheter rebbe's brother. He was weeping bitterly. I thought he was crying with joy at still being alive.

20 "Don't cry, Yehiel," I said. "Don't waste your tears . . ."

21 "Not cry? We're on the threshold of death. Soon, we shall be inside . . . Do you understand? Inside. How could I not cry?"

22 I watched darkness fade through the bluish skylights in the roof. I no longer was afraid. I was overcome by fatigue.

23 The absent no longer entered our thoughts. One spoke of them—who knows what happened to them?—but their fate was not on our minds. We were

NOTES

incapable of thinking. Our senses were numbed, everything was fading into a fog. We no longer clung to anything. The instincts of self-preservation, of self-defense, of pride, had all deserted us. In one terrifying moment of lucidity, I thought of us as damned souls wandering through the void, souls condemned to wander through space until the end of time, seeking **redemption,** seeking oblivion, without any hope of finding either.

24   Around five o'clock in the morning, we were expelled from the barrack. The Kapos were beating us again, but I no longer felt the pain. A glacial wind was enveloping us. We were naked, holding our shoes and belts. An order:

25   "Run!" And we ran. After a few minutes of running, a new barrack.

26   A barrel of foul-smelling liquid stood by the door. Disinfection. Everybody soaked in it. Then came a hot shower. All very fast. As we left the showers, we were chased outside. And ordered to run some more. Another barrack: the storeroom. Very long tables. Mountains of prison garb. As we ran, they threw the clothes at us: pants, jackets, shirts. . .

27   In a few seconds, we had ceased to be men. Had the situation not been so tragic, we might have laughed. We looked pretty strange! Meir Katz, a colossus, wore a child's pants, and Stern, a skinny little fellow, was floundering in a huge jacket. We immediately started to switch.

28   I glanced over at my father. How changed he looked! His eyes were veiled. I wanted to tell him something, but I didn't know what.

29   The night had passed completely. The morning star shone in the sky. I too had become a different person. The student of Talmud, the child I was, had been consumed by the flames. All that was left was a shape that resembled me. My soul had been invaded—and devoured—by a black flame.

30   So many events had taken place in just a few hours that I had completely lost all notion of time. When had we left our homes? And the ghetto? And the train? Only a week ago? One night? One single night?

31   How long had we been standing in the freezing wind? One hour? A single hour? Sixty minutes?

32   Surely it was a dream.

Excerpted from *Night* by Elie Wiesel, published by Hill and Wang.

THINK QUESTIONS CA-CCSS: CA.RI.9-10.1, CA.RI.9-10.4, CA.L.9-10.4a, CA.L.9-10.4b

1. At the beginning of the passage, how does author Elie Wiesel say his first night at the camp affected him? How would you characterize the language he uses? Support your answer with evidence from the text.

2. What are conditions like in the camp? Include evidence from the text in your answer.

3. What can readers infer about Wiesel's relationship with his father? Support your answer with textual evidence.

4. Use context clues in the passage to determine the meaning of **antechamber**. Write your definition of "antechamber" here and tell how you got it.

5. Use context to determine the meaning of the word **interspersed** as it is used in the passage. Write your definition of "interspersed" here and tell how you found it.

CLOSE READ

CA-CCSS: CA.RI.9-10.1, CA.RI.9-10.2, CA.RI.9-10.3, CA.RI.9-10.4, CA.RI.9-10.5, CA.RI.9-10.6, CA.W.9-10.1, CA.W.9-10.1a, CA.W.9-10.1b, CA.W.9-10.4, CA.W.9-10.5, CA.W.9-10.6, CA.W.9-10.9b, CA.W.9-10.10

Reread the excerpt from *Night*. As you reread, complete the Focus Questions below. Then use your answers and annotations from the questions to help you complete the Writing Prompt.

FOCUS QUESTIONS

1. Explain the effect on the reader of the section that repeats the word "never." What does this section contribute to the overall mood and tone of the excerpt? Highlight evidence from the text and make annotations to explain your choices.

2. What do the actions and reactions of other inmates suggest about life in the camp? Support your answer with textual evidence and make annotations to explain your answer choices.

3. How does Elie Wiesel use paragraph and sentence structure to mirror his thinking? What effect does this have on the reader? Use the annotation tool to highlight your textual evidence and make annotations to explain your choices.

4. As Elie Wiesel reveals the series of events that he endured, what conclusions does he draw? Cite details from the passage to explain how Wiesel's experiences affect his thinking.

5. In what way does the experience of surviving the death camps now define Wiesel? Highlight textual evidence and make annotations to explain your choices.

WRITING PROMPT

The author keeps a mental catalog of things he "never shall forget." In an essay of at least 300 words, explore why Wiesel maintains these painful memories. Do you agree that he should keep them intact? What would he lose by forgetting them? In your essay, touch on how Wiesel uses tone to support his position.

Please note that excerpts and passages in the StudySync® library and this workbook are intended as touchstones to generate interest in an author's work. The excerpts and passages do not substitute for the reading of entire texts, and StudySync® strongly recommends that students seek out and purchase the whole literary or informational work in order to experience it as the author intended. Links to online resellers are available in our digital library. In addition, complete works may be ordered through an authorized reseller by filling out and returning to StudySync® the order form enclosed in this workbook.

Reading & Writing Companion   **41**

HOTEL RWANDA

DRAMA
Keir Pearson and Terry George
2004

INTRODUCTION

Based on real-life events of the Rwandan civil war between the Hutu and Tutsi ethnic groups, *Hotel Rwanda* dramatizes the heroic actions of Paul Rusesabagina, who is credited with hiding and saving over 1,000 people at the hotel he managed in the Rwandan capital of Kigali. In this excerpt from Keir Pearson and Terry George's screenplay, civil war has erupted, and the situation at Hotel Mille Collines is dangerous and chaotic.

"There will be no rescue. No intervention force. We can only save ourselves."

 ## FIRST READ

NOTES

INT. SABENA OFFICES – BELGIUM – TILLEN'S OFFICE – DAY

1 *The Sabena President and three VPs have an early morning meeting. The intercom buzzes.*

2 TILLENS: Yes?

3 SECRETARY (V.O. – THRU SPEAKER PHONE): Sorry, sir, but I have a call from Paul in Kigali. He says it's urgent.

4 *The President hits the speaker button.*

5 TILLENS: Paul. Are you all right?

6 PAUL (V.O. – THRU SPEAKER PHONE): We have a big problem, sir.

7 TILLENS: What?

8 PAUL (V.O. – THRU SPEAKER PHONE): The Hutu Army have come. They've ordered us – all of us – out of the hotel.

9 TILLENS: Why are they doing this?

10 PAUL (V.O. – THRU SPEAKER PHONE): I think they will kill us all.

11 TILLENS (*stunned*): Kill? What do you mean ... all? How many?

12 PAUL (V.O. – THRU SPEAKER PHONE): We have one hundred staff, and now more than eight hundred guests.

13 *Tillens can barely form words to reply.*

14 TILLENS: Eight hundred!

Please note that excerpts and passages in the StudySync® library and this workbook are intended as touchstones to generate interest in an author's work. The excerpts and passages do not substitute for the reading of entire texts, and StudySync® strongly recommends that students seek out and purchase the whole literary or informational work in order to experience it as the author intended. Links to online resellers are available in our digital library. In addition, complete works may be ordered through an authorized reseller by filling out and returning to StudySync® the order form enclosed in this workbook.

Reading & Writing Companion **43**

Copyright © BookheadEd Learning, LLC

NOTES

15   PAUL (V.O. – THRU SPEAKER PHONE): Yes, sir. There are now eight hundred Tutsi and Hutu refugees. I do not have much time left, sir. I want to thank you for everything you have done for me and my family, and please thank all of my friends at Sabena.

16   *The President considers this.*

17   TILLENS: Paul, wait. I'm gonna put you on hold. Stay by the phone.

18   *He hits the hold button, looks to the other executives. They are stunned to silence by Paul's profound farewell.*

INT. HOTEL MILLE COLLINES – MANAGER'S OFFICE – DAY

19   *Paul sits in the office, his hand over the mouthpiece. From the lobby come soldiers' angry voices.*

20   SOLDIER (O.S.): Where are your papers?

INT. SABENA OFFICES – BELGIUM – TILLEN'S OFFICE – DAY

21   *The President gets everyone working on the phone.*

22   TILLENS: Louis, get on to the UN. Tell them what's happening. Mary, call the Prime Minister's office. Tell them I must speak with him now.

23   *The President lifts the telephone receiver and hits a button.*

24   TILLENS: Paul, are you there?

25   PAUL (V.O. – THRU SPEAKER PHONE): Yes, sir.

26   TILLENS: Who can I call to stop this?

27   *Paul thinks.*

28   PAUL (V.O. – THRU SPEAKER PHONE): The French – they supply the Hutu Army.

29   TILLENS: Do everything you can to bide time. I'll call you right back.

30   *Paul hurries from the room.*

INT. HOTEL MILLE COLLINES – LOBBY – DAY

31   *Dube is at the computer, printing something. Paul walks quickly to him.*

32   PAUL: What are you doing, Dube?

NOTES

33 DUBE: The Lieutenant, sir. He wants to see the guest list.

34 *Paul nervously glances at the soldiers.*

35 PAUL: Go and get these boys some more beer.

36 *Dube walks to the bar to get the beer, and Paul is on the computer, typing. A receptionist looks at the screen.*

37 RECEPTIONIST: Sir, that guest list is from two weeks ago.

38 PAUL: Shh.

39 *Paul hits the print button. The printer clicks to life.*

INT. HOTEL MILLE COLLINES – ENTRANCE – DAY

40 *Paul emerges with the printed registry. The Lieutenant marches up to Paul.*

41 HUTU LIEUTENANT: Where's the guest list?

42 *Paul hands him the print out. The Lieutenant studies it.*

43 HUTU LIEUTENANT: Anderson, Arthurs, Boulier... What is this?

44 PAUL: It is the guest list, sir.

45 HUTU LIEUTENANT: Are you trying to make a fool out of me?

46 PAUL: No. We stopped taking names after the President was murdered. This is the only guest list, sir.

47 HUTU LIEUTENANT: There are no Europeans left. Get me the names of all the cockroaches in there, now.

48 PAUL: That will take time.

49 HUTU LIEUTENANT: You don't have time. If I don't have the names so that I can pick out the traitors, then I'll kill everyone in there. Starting with you.

50 *The Lieutenant's radio comes to life and he turns to answer it. He listens for a moment...*

51 HUTU LIEUTENANT (INTO RADIO): Yes, sir?

52 *He angrily turns to Paul and grabs him.*

53 HUTU LIEUTENANT: Who did you call?

Copyright © BookheadEd Learning, LLC

NOTES

54 PAUL: Who did I call?

55 HUTU LIEUTENANT: Don't lie to me! What is your name?

56 PAUL: Rusesabagina. Paul Rusesabagina.

57 HUTU LIEUTENANT: I'll remember you.

58 *He prods Paul's chest.*

59 HUTU LIEUTENANT (CONT'D): I'll remember you.

60 *He turns to his soldiers, gestures.*

61 HUTU LIEUTENANT (CONT'D): Let's go.

62 *They drive off.*

INT. HOTEL MILLE COLLINES – ROOF – DAY

63 *Paul emerges onto the roof. He looks around for his family, sees Tatiana, his children and the neighbors sitting huddled together.*

64 PAUL: They've gone.

65 TATIANA: Oh.

66 *Tatiana grabs him.*

67 TATIANA (CONT'D): I was so afraid for you.

68 *Dube appears.*

69 DUBE: Sir, the President of Sabena is on the phone for you.

70 *Paul strokes Tatiana's face.*

71 PAUL: I must talk with this man.

INT. HOTEL MILLE COLLINES – MANAGER'S OFFICE – DAY

72 *Paul hits the button and lifts the telephone receiver.*

73 PAUL: Mr. Tillens.

74 TILLENS (V.O. – THRU PHONE): Paul, what's going on?

75 *Paul shakes his head in disbelief.*

76   PAUL: They left. Thank you, sir. What did you do?

INT. SABENA OFFICES – BELGIUM – TILLEN'S OFFICE – DAY

77   *The Sabena President is at his desk.*

78   TILLENS: I got through to the French President's office.

79   PAUL (V.O. – THRU SPEAKER PHONE): Well, thank you. You have saved our lives.

80   TILLENS: I pleaded with the French and the Belgians to go back and get you all. I'm afraid this is not going to happen.

81   *Silence, Tillens is ashamed, angry.*

82   TILLENS (CONT'D): They're cowards, Paul. Rwanda is not – worth a single vote to any of them. The French, the British, the Americans. I am sorry, Paul.

INT. HOTEL MILLE COLLINES – MANAGER'S OFFICE – DAY

83   *Paul is stunned.*

84   PAUL: Thank you.

INT. HOTEL MILLE COLLINES – FUNCTION ROOM – DAY

85   *The refugees are gathered, Paul addresses them.*

86   PAUL: There will be no rescue. No intervention force. We can only save ourselves. Many of you know influential people abroad. You must call these people.

INT. HOTEL MILLE COLLINES – MANAGER'S OFFICE – DAY

87   *MONTAGE of influential refugees. Odette, Benedict, Xavier call, plead, write and send faxes.*

88   *Odette sits at the desk, on the phone.*

89   PAUL (V.O.): You must tell them what will happen to us.

90   *Other refugees are on the phones.*

91   PAUL (V.O. CONT'D): Say goodbye. But when you say goodbye, say it as though you are reaching through the phone and holding their hand. Let them know that if they let go of that hand... you will die. We must shame them into

sending help. Most importantly, this can not be a refugee camp. The Interahamwe believe that the Mille Collines is a four-star Sabena hotel. That is the only thing keeping us alive.

INT. HOTEL MILLE COLLINES – LOBBY – DAY

92   *Paul on the move, organizing, walks to the receptionist at the front desk.*

93   PAUL: Have you printed the bills?

94   *She hands him a stack of envelopes.*

95   PAUL (CONT'D): Now please erase the registry.

96   RECEPTIONIST: Erase it?

97   PAUL: Yes. I want no names to appear there.

98   *Dube joins him.*

99   DUBE: Boss, the carpenters are ready.

100   PAUL: Tell them to remove all of the numbers from the doors.

101   DUBE: And put what?

102   PAUL: And put nothing.

INT. HOTEL MILLE COLLINES – HALLWAY – DAY

103   *Paul goes door to door, knocking. The rooms are all packed with Tutsi refugees. A door opens. He hands an envelope to the refugee.*

104   PAUL: Good day. Here is your bill for the last week. If you cannot pay, or think you will not be able to pay, please go to the banquet room and Dube will take care of you. Thank you.

INT. HOTEL MILLE COLLINES – GROUNDS – NIGHT

105   *Refugees are clustered on the ground, in tents, as the radio voice plays over a reporter's interview of a State Department Officer.*

106   AMERICAN REPORTER (V.O. – THRU RADIO): Does the State Department have a view as to whether or not what is happening – could be genocide?

107   STATE DEPARTMENT OFFICER (V.O. – THRU RADIO): We have every reason to believe that acts of genocide have occurred.

108 *Inside his office Paul and the others listen.*

109 BRITISH REPORTER (V.O. – THRU RADIO): How many acts of genocide does it take to make genocide?

110 STATE DEPARTMENT OFFICER (V.O. – THRU RADIO): Alan, that's not a question that I'm in a position to answer.

111 BRITISH REPORTER (V.O. – THRU RADIO): Is it true that you have specific guidance not to use the word genocide in isolation, but always to preface it with this word, "acts of"?

112 STATE DEPARTMENT OFFICER (V.O. – THRU RADIO): I have guidance which I try to use as best I can. There are formulations that we are using that we are trying to be consistent in our use of.

113 *Paul is listening to all of this. Benedict turns off the radio in disgust.*

---

pp. 71–9 from HOTEL RWANDA by TERRY GEORGE and KEIR PEARSON. Compilation copyright (c) 2005 by Newmarket Press. Used by permission of HarperCollins Publishers.

☁ THINK QUESTIONS CA-CCSS: CA.RL.9-10.1, CA.RL.9-10.4, CA.L.9-10.4a

1. Use two or more details from the text to describe Paul. What details in the screenplay help you get a sense of his character?

2. Sabena's president, Mr. Tillens, attempts to secure immediate help for Paul and the eight hundred refugees. Whom does Tillens contact and what is the ultimate result for Paul and the refugees hiding in the hotel? Cite text evidence to support your answer.

3. Why does Paul go to such elaborate measures to try and convince the Hutu lieutenant that most of the guests at the Mille Collines Hotel are Europeans? Use evidence from the text to support your answer.

4. Based on the text, what does the word **registry** mean? Explain which context clues help you arrive at a definition.

5. Use context to determine the meaning of the word **intervention** as it is used within the text. Write your definition of "intervention" here and tell how you found it.

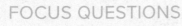 **CLOSE READ** CA-CCSS: CA.RL.9-10.1, CA.RL.9-10.3, CA.RL.9-10.5, CA.RL.9-10.4, CA.W.9-10.2a, CA.W.9-10.2b, CA.W.9-10.4, CA.W.9-10.5, CA.W.9-10.6, CA.W.9-10.9a, CA.W.9-10.10

Reread the excerpt from Hotel Rwanda. As you reread, complete the Focus Questions below. Then use your answers and annotations from the questions to help you complete the Writing Prompt.

FOCUS QUESTIONS

1. During the montage sequence in the manager's office, Paul is heard in voiceover as the screen shows a number of influential refugees—Odette, Benedict, and Xavier—calling and sending faxes. At one point, Paul says, "this cannot be a refugee camp. The Interahamwe believe that the Mille Collines is a four-star Sabena hotel. That is the only thing keeping us alive." What does he mean by this, and what does it have to do with the fact that Paul is handing bills out to the refugees hiding in the rooms? Highlight evidence from the text to support your answers

2. The second time Paul speaks to Mr. Tillens in Belgium, the president of Sabena tells Paul that, although he pleaded with the French and the Belgians to go in and rescue the refugees at the hotel, they refused to do so. This time, as Paul receives the news, the scene shifts from Belgium back to Rwanda so the camera can record Paul's reaction. Why do you think the screenwriters elected to do this, when in his previous conversation with Tillens Paul was heard only in voiceover?

3. A very general rule in filmmaking is that a page in the screenplay should equal about a minute of screen time. Make a print out of the screenplay excerpt on your computer. How many pages is it? Then reread the excerpt and determine how many scenes and locations it contains. How much real time does the excerpt cover in the story, and how long would it actually last in screen time?

4. At the end of the selection, Benedict, one of the influential refugees, is listening to the radio with Paul. A British reporter is interviewing a state department officer about the situation in Rwanda. Why does Benedict turn off the radio in disgust? Use evidence from the text to support your answer.

5. In what way does the radio broadcast that Paul and Benedict listen to at the end of the excerpt reinforce what Mr. Tillens had told Paul earlier? Use evidence from the text to support your answer.

WRITING PROMPT

This screenplay is set in the rooms and grounds of the Hotel Mille Collines in Rwanda, as well as in the office of Sabena president Tillens. Yet the title of the film is *Hotel Rwanda,* even though a hotel with this name is never mentioned in the excerpt. Based on the way screenwriters Keir Pearson and Terry George have structured the events in the screenplay, why do you think they chose this title? In what way can the Mille Collines be seen as a microcosm for what is taking place in all of Rwanda? Cite evidence from the text in your answer.

DOVER BEACH

POETRY
Matthew Arnold
1867

INTRODUCTION

Considered by some to be the first distinctly modern poem, the inspiration for Matthew Arnold's "Dover Beach" was likely a honeymoon trip to the English port city of Dover. Perhaps speaking to wife, Arnold writes about the beauty of nature, and notes the conflicts between science and faith

"Ah, love, let us be true"

NOTES

 FIRST READ

1   The sea is calm to-night.

2   The tide is full, the moon lies fair

3   Upon the straits; on the French coast the light

4   Gleams and is gone; the cliffs of England stand;

5   Glimmering and vast, out in the **tranquil** bay.

6   Come to the window, sweet is the night-air!

7   Only, from the long line of spray

8   Where the sea meets the moon-**blanched** land,

9   Listen! you hear the grating roar

10 Of pebbles which the waves draw back, and fling,

11 At their return, up the high strand,

12 Begin, and cease, and then again begin,

13 With **tremulous cadence** slow, and bring

14 The eternal note of sadness in.

15 Sophocles long ago

16 Heard it on the Agaean, and it brought

17 Into his mind the turbid ebb and flow

18 Of human misery; we

19 Find also in the sound a thought,

20 Hearing it by this distant northern sea.

21 The Sea of Faith

22 Was once, too, at the full, and round earth's shore

23 Lay like the folds of a bright girdle furled.

24 But now I only hear

25 Its melancholy, long, withdrawing roar,

26 Retreating, to the breath

27 Of the night-wind, down the vast edges drear

28 And naked shingles of the world.

29 Ah, love, let us be true

30 To one another! for the world, which seems

31 To lie before us like a land of dreams,

32 So various, so beautiful, so new,

33 Hath really neither joy, nor love, nor light,

34 Nor **certitude,** nor peace, nor help for pain;

35 And we are here as on a darkling plain

36 Swept with confused alarms of struggle and flight,

37 Where ignorant armies clash by night.

THINK QUESTIONS  CA-CCSS: CA.RL.9-10.1, CA.RL.9-10.4, CA.L.9-10.4a

1. What contrast is established in the first stanza of the poem? What emotional effect does the scene have on the speaker? Use text evidence to support your answer.

2. The second stanza of the poem contains an allusion to Sophocles, an ancient Greek dramatist whose tragedies are still read widely today. How is this reference to Sophocles used to make a point about the human condition?

3. How does the speaker in this poem view the world, according to text evidence in the poem?

4. Use context to determine the meaning of the word **tranquil** as it is used in the first stanza of *Dover Beach*. Write your definition of "tranquil" here and tell how you arrived at it.

5. Use context to determine the meaning of the word **cadence** as it is used in the final stanza of *Dover Beach*. Write your definition of "cadence" here and tell how you arrived at it.

Please note that excerpts and passages in the StudySync® library and this workbook are intended as touchstones to generate interest in an author's work. The excerpts and passages do not substitute for the reading of entire texts, and StudySync® strongly recommends that students seek out and purchase the whole literary or informational work in order to experience it as the author intended. Links to online resellers are available in our digital library. In addition, complete works may be ordered through an authorized reseller by filling out and returning to StudySync® the order form enclosed in this workbook.

Reading & Writing
Companion

53

CLOSE READ
CA-CCSS: CA.RL.9-10.1, CA.RL.9-10.2, CA.RL.9-10.4, CA.RL.9-10.10, CA.W.9-10.2a, CA.W.9-10.5, CA.W.9-10.6, CA.W.9-10.9a, CA.W.9-10.10, CA.L.9-10.5a, CA.W.9-10.2b, CA.W.9-10.4

Reread the poem "Dover Beach." As you reread, complete the Focus Questions below. Then use your answers and annotations from the questions to help you complete the Writing Prompt.

FOCUS QUESTIONS

1. Explore the metaphorical significance of the ocean tides in the first two stanzas of the poem. For what are the waves a metaphor? How do words with strong connotations help develop the metaphor?

2. How do the speaker's religious beliefs—or lack of them—influence the way he looks upon and reacts to the scene on Dover Beach? How does the speaker view the human condition?

3. Describe the denotations and connotations of the words in the final stanza. Tell how they are used to develop the overall theme of the poem.

4. What role does the listener in the poem play? How do the speaker's interactions with this person help define his character?

5. What insight does this poem offer about how an individual's interactions with nature may help define his or her character?

WRITING PROMPT

After reading Arnold's poem, think of a place in nature that has had a powerful effect on you. In a well-developed essay, describe that place in detail, using words with strong connotations and precise denotations. Explain what emotions the place inspires in you and why, as well as what insight viewing it might offer about life, faith, the human condition, or humanity's relationship with nature. What metaphorical significance might this place have? Compare your response to your place to the way Arnold responds to the beach in his poem, analyzing in particular how each of you uses words with strong connotations as well as denotations to set the tone and develop theme.

CATCH THE MOON

FICTION

Judith Ortiz Cofer
1995

INTRODUCTION

studysync tv

ailing from a family of storytellers, Judith Ortiz Cofer is a Puerto Rican-born author of award-winning poetry, short stories, essays, and a memoir. She is also a professor of English and Creative Writing at the University of Georgia. Her poems and short stories explore cultural differences and draw upon her experiences as a Latina immigrant, and she has said, "I write in English, yet I write obsessively about my Puerto Rican experience." The selection here, "Catch the Moon," comes from *An Island Like You: Stories of the Barrio*, a book of short stories for young adults.

"Someday, son, all this will be yours..."

 FIRST READ

1   Luis Cintrón sits on top of a six-foot pile of hubcaps and watches his father walk away into the steel jungle of his car junkyard. Released into his old man's custody after six months in juvenile hall—for breaking and entering—and he didn't even take anything. He did it on a dare. But the old lady with the million cats was a light sleeper, and good with her aluminum cane. He has a scar on his head to prove it.

2   Now Luis is wondering whether he should have stayed in and done his full time. Jorge Cintrón of Jorge Cintrón & Son, Auto Parts and Salvage, has decided that Luis should wash and polish every hubcap in the yard. The hill he is sitting on is only the latest couple of hundred wheel covers that have come in. Luis grunts and stands up on top of his silver mountain. He yells at no one, "Someday, son, all this will be yours," and sweeps his arms like the Pope blessing a crowd over the piles of car sandwiches and mounds of metal parts that cover this acre of land outside the city. He is the "Son" of Jorge Cintrón & Son, and so far his father has had more than one reason to wish it was plain Jorge Cintrón on the sign.

3   Luis has been getting in trouble since he started high school two years ago, mainly because of the "social group" he organized—a bunch of guys who were into harassing the local authorities. Their thing was taking something to the limit on a dare or, better still, doing something dangerous, like breaking into a house, not to steal, just to prove that they could do it. This was Luis's specialty, coming up with very complicated plans, like military strategies, and assigning the "jobs" to guys who wanted to join the Tiburones.

4   *Tiburón* means "shark," and Luis had gotten the name from watching an old movie about a Puerto Rican gang called the Sharks with his father. Luis thought it was one of the dumbest films he had ever seen. Everybody sang their lines, and the guys all pointed their toes and leaped in the air when they

NOTES

were supposed to be slaughtering each other. But he liked their name, the Sharks, so he made it Spanish and had it air-painted on his black T-shirt with a killer shark under it, jaws opened wide and dripping with blood. It didn't take long for other guys in the barrio to ask about it.

5   Man, had they had a good time. The girls were interested too. Luis outsmarted everybody by calling his organization a social club and registering it at Central High. That meant they were legal, even let out of last-period class on Fridays for their "club" meetings. It was just this year, after a couple of **botched** jobs, that the teachers had started getting suspicious. The first one to go wrong was when he sent Kenny Matoa to *borrow* some "souvenirs" out of Anita Robles's locker. He got caught. It seems that Matoa had been reading Anita's diary and didn't hear her coming down the hall. Anita was supposed to be in the gym at that time but had copped out with the usual female excuse of cramps. You could hear her screams all the way to Market Street.

6   She told the principal all she knew about the Tiburones, and Luis had to talk fast to convince old Mr.Williams that the club did put on cultural activities such as the Save the Animals talent show. What Mr.Williams didn't know was that the animal that was being "saved" with the ticket sales was Luis's pet boa, which needed quite a few live mice to stay healthy and happy. They kept E. S. (which stood for "Endangered Species") in Luis's room, but she belonged to the club and it was the members' responsibility to raise the money to feed their mascot. So last year they had sponsored their first annual Save the Animals talent show, and it had been a great success. The Tiburones had come dressed as Latino Elvises and did a grand finale to "All Shook Up" that made the audience go wild. Mr.Williams had smiled while Luis talked, maybe remembering how the math teacher, Mrs. Laguna, had dragged him out in the aisle to rock-and-roll with her. Luis had gotten out of that one, but barely.

7   His father was a problem, too. He objected to the T-shirt logo, calling it disgusting and **vulgar.** Mr. Cintrón prided himself on his own neat, elegant style of dressing after work, and on his manners and large vocabulary, which he picked up by taking correspondence courses in just about everything. Luis thought it was just his way of staying busy since Luis's mother had died, almost three years ago, of cancer. He had never gotten over it.

8   All this was going through Luis's head as he slid down the hill of hubcaps. The tub full of soapy water, the can of polish, and the bag of rags had been neatly placed in front of a makeshift table made from two car seats and a piece of plywood. Luis heard a car drive up and someone honk their horn. His father emerged from inside a new red Mustang that had been totaled. He usually **dismantled** every small feature by hand before sending the vehicle into the *cementerio,* as he called the lot. Luis watched as the most beautiful girl he had ever seen climbed out of a **vintage** white Volkswagen Bug. She stood in

the sunlight in her white sundress waiting for his father, while Luis stared. She was like a smooth wood carving. Her skin was mahogany, almost black, and her arms and legs were long and thin, but curved in places so that she did not look bony and hard—more like a ballerina. And her ebony hair was braided close to her head. Luis let his breath out, feeling a little dizzy. He had forgotten to breathe. Both the girl and his father heard him. Mr. Cintrón waved him over.

9   "Luis, the señorita here has lost a wheel cover. Her car is twenty-five years old, so it will not be an easy match. Come look on this side."

10 Luis tossed a wrench he'd been holding into a toolbox like he was annoyed, just to make a point about slave labor. Then he followed his father, who knelt on the gravel and began to point out every detail of the hubcap. Luis was hardly listening. He watched the girl take a piece of paper from her handbag.

11 "Señor Cintrón, I have drawn the hubcap for you, since I will have to leave soon. My home address and telephone number are here, and also my parents' office number." She handed the paper to Mr. Cintrón, who nodded.

12 "Sí, señorita, very good. This will help my son look for it. Perhaps there is one in that stack there." He pointed to the pile of caps that Luis was supposed to wash and polish. "Yes, I'm almost certain that there is a match there. Of course, I do not know if it's near the top or the bottom. You will give us a few days, yes?"

13 Luis just stared at his father like he was crazy. But he didn't say anything because the girl was smiling at him with a funny expression on her face. Maybe she thought he had X-ray eyes like Superman, or maybe she was mocking him.

14 "Please call me Naomi, Señor Cintrón. You know my mother. She is the director of the funeral home. . . ." Mr. Cintrón seemed surprised at first; he prided himself on having a great memory. Then his friendly expression changed to one of sadness as he recalled the day of his wife's burial. Naomi did not finish her sentence. She reached over and placed her hand on Mr. Cintrón's arm for a moment. Then she said "Adiós" softly, and got in her shiny white car. She waved to them as she left, and her gold bracelets flashing in the sun nearly blinded Luis.

15 Mr. Cintrón shook his head. "How about that," he said as if to himself. "They are the Dominican owners of Ramirez Funeral Home." And, with a sigh, "She seems like such a nice young woman. Reminds me of your mother when she was her age."

16 Hearing the funeral parlor's name, Luis remembered too. The day his mother died, he had been in her room at the hospital while his father had gone for

NOTES

coffee. The alarm had gone off on her monitor and nurses had come running in, pushing him outside. After that, all he recalled was the anger that had made him punch a hole in his bedroom wall. And afterward he had refused to talk to anyone at the funeral. Strange, he did see a black girl there who didn't try like the others to talk to him, but actually ignored him as she escorted family members to the viewing room and brought flowers in. Could it be that the skinny girl in a frilly white dress had been Naomi? She didn't act like she had recognized him today, though. Or maybe she thought that he was a jerk.

17 Luis grabbed the drawing from his father. The old man looked like he wanted to walk down memory lane. But Luis was in no mood to listen to the old stories about his falling in love on a tropical island. The world they'd lived in before he was born wasn't his world. No beaches and palm trees here. Only junk as far as he could see. He climbed back up his hill and studied Naomi's sketch. It had obviously been done very carefully. It was signed "Naomi Ramirez" in the lower right-hand corner. He memorized the telephone number.

18 Luis washed hubcaps all day until his hands were red and raw, but he did not come across the small silver bowl that would fit the VW. After work he took a few practice Frisbee shots across the yard before showing his father what he had accomplished: rows and rows of shiny rings drying in the sun. His father nodded and showed him the bump on his temple where one of Luis's flying saucers had gotten him. "Practice makes perfect, you know. Next time you'll probably **decapitate** me." Luis heard him struggle with the word *decapitate,* which Mr. Cintrón pronounced in syllables. Showing off his big vocabulary again, Luis thought. He looked closely at the bump, though. He felt bad about it.

19 "They look good, hijo," Mr. Cintrón made a sweeping gesture with his arms over the yard. "You know, all this will have to be classified. My dream is to have all the parts divided by year, make of car, and condition. Maybe now that you are here to help me, this will happen."

20 "Pop . . ." Luis put his hand on his father's shoulder. They were the same height and build, about five foot six and muscular. "The judge said six months of free labor for you, not life, okay?" Mr. Cintrón nodded, looking distracted. It was then that Luis suddenly noticed how gray his hair had turned—it used to be shiny black like his own—and that there were deep lines in his face. His father had turned into an old man and he hadn't even noticed.

21 "Son, you must follow the judge's instructions. Like she said, next time you get in trouble, she's going to treat you like an adult, and I think you know what that means. Hard time, no breaks."

NOTES

22 "Yeah, yeah. That's what I'm doing, right? Working my hands to the bone instead of enjoying my summer. But listen, she didn't put me under house arrest, right? I'm going out tonight."

23 "Home by ten. She did say something about a curfew, Luis." Mr. Cintrón had stopped smiling and was looking upset. It had always been hard for them to talk more than a minute or two before his father got offended at something Luis said, or at his sarcastic tone. He was always doing something wrong. Luis threw the rag down on the table and went to sit in his father's ancient Buick, which was in mint condition. They drove home in silence.

24 After sitting down at the kitchen table with his father to eat a pizza they had picked up on the way home, Luis asked to borrow the car. He didn't get an answer then, just a look that meant "Don't bother me right now."

25 Before bringing up the subject again, Luis put some ice cubes in a Baggie and handed it to Mr. Cintrón, who had made the little bump on his head worse by rubbing it. It had GUILTY written on it, Luis thought.

26 "Gracias, hijo." His father placed the bag on the bump and made a face as the ice touched his skin.

27 They ate in silence for a few minutes more; then Luis decided to ask about the car again.

28 "I really need some fresh air, Pop. Can I borrow the car for a couple of hours?"

29 "You don't get enough fresh air at the yard? We're lucky that we don't have to sit in a smelly old factory all day. You know that?"

30 "Yeah, Pop. We're real lucky." Luis always felt irritated that his father was so grateful to own a junkyard, but he held his anger back and just waited to see if he'd get the keys without having to get in an argument.

31 "Where are you going?"

32 "For a ride. Not going anywhere. Just out for a while. Is that okay?"

33 His father didn't answer, just handed him a set of keys, as shiny as the day they were manufactured. His father polished everything that could be polished: doorknobs, coins, keys, spoons, knives, and forks, like he was King Midas counting his silver and gold. Luis thought his father must be really lonely to polish utensils only he used anymore. They had been picked out by his wife, though, so they were like relics. Nothing she had ever owned could be thrown away. Only now the dishes, forks, and spoons were not used to eat the yellow rice and red beans, the fried chicken, or the mouth-watering sweet

plantains that his mother had cooked for them. They were just kept in the cabinets that his father had turned into a museum for her. Mr. Cintrón could cook as well as his wife, but he didn't have the heart to do it anymore. Luis thought that maybe if they ate together once in a while things might get better between them, but he always had something to do around dinnertime and ended up at a hamburger joint. Tonight was the first time in months they had sat down at the table together.

34 Luis took the keys. "Thanks," he said, walking out to take his shower. His father kept looking at him with those sad, patient eyes. "Okay. I'll be back by ten, and keep the ice on that egg," Luis said without looking back.

35 He had just meant to ride around his old barrio, see if any of the Tiburones were hanging out at El Building, where most of them lived. It wasn't far from the single-family home his father had bought when the business starting paying off: a house that his mother lived in for three months before she took up residence at St. Joseph's Hospital. She never came home again. These days Luis wished he still lived in that tiny apartment where there was always something to do, somebody to talk to.

36 Instead Luis found himself parked in front of the last place his mother had gone to: Ramirez Funeral Home. In the front yard was a huge oak tree that Luis remembered having climbed during the funeral to get away from people. The tree looked different now, not like a skeleton as it had then, but green with leaves. The branches reached to the second floor of the house, where the family lived.

37 For a while Luis sat in the car allowing the memories to flood back into his brain. He remembered his mother before the illness changed her. She had not been beautiful, as his father told everyone; she had been a sweet lady, not pretty but not ugly. To him, she had been the person who always told him that she was proud of him and loved him. She did that every night when she came to his bedroom door to say goodnight. As a joke he would sometimes ask her, "Proud of what? I haven't done anything." And she'd always say, "I'm just proud that you are my son." She wasn't perfect or anything. She had bad days when nothing he did could make her smile, especially after she got sick. But he never heard her say anything negative about anyone. She always blamed *el destino,* fate, for what went wrong. He missed her. He missed her so much. Suddenly a flood of tears that had been building up for almost three years started pouring from his eyes. Luis sat in his father's car, with his head on the steering wheel, and cried, "Mami, I miss you."

38 When he finally looked up, he saw that he was being watched. Sitting at a large window with a pad and a pencil on her lap was Naomi. At first Luis felt angry and embarrassed, but she wasn't laughing at him. Then she told him

with her dark eyes that it was okay to come closer. He walked to the window, and she held up the sketch pad on which she had drawn him, not crying like a baby, but sitting on top of a mountain of silver disks, holding one up over his head. He had to smile.

39   The plate-glass window was locked. It had a security bolt on it. An alarm system, he figured, so nobody would steal the princess. He asked her if he could come in. It was soundproof too. He mouthed the words slowly for her to read his lips. She wrote on the pad, "I can't let you in. My mother is not home tonight." So they looked at each other and talked through the window for a little while. Then Luis got an idea. He signed to her that he'd be back, and drove to the junkyard.

40   Luis climbed up on his mountain of hubcaps. For hours he sorted the wheel covers by make, size, and condition, stopping only to call his father and tell him where he was and what he was doing. The old man did not ask him for explanations, and Luis was grateful for that. By lamppost light, Luis worked and worked, beginning to understand a little why his father kept busy all the time. Doing something that had a beginning, a middle, and an end did something to your head. It was like the satisfaction Luis got out of planning "adventures" for his Tiburones, but there was another element involved here that had nothing to do with showing off for others. This was a treasure hunt. And he knew what he was looking for.

41   Finally, when it seemed that it was a hopeless search, when it was almost midnight and Luis's hands were cut and bruised from his work, he found it. It was the perfect match for Naomi's drawing, the moon-shaped wheel cover for her car, Cinderella's shoe. Luis jumped off the small mound of disks left under him and shouted, "Yes!" He looked around and saw neat stacks of hubcaps that he would wash the next day. He would build a display wall for his father. People would be able to come into the yard and point to whatever they wanted.

42   Luis washed the VW hubcap and polished it until he could see himself in it. He used it as a mirror as he washed his face and combed his hair. Then he drove to the Ramirez Funeral Home. It was almost pitch-black, since it was a moonless night. As quietly as possible, Luis put some gravel in his pocket and climbed the oak tree to the second floor. He knew he was in front of Naomi's window—he could see her shadow through the curtains. She was at a table, apparently writing or drawing, maybe waiting for him. Luis hung the silver disk carefully on a branch near the window, then threw the gravel at the glass. Naomi ran to the window and drew the curtains aside while Luis held on to the thick branch and waited to give her the first good thing he had given anyone in a long time.

THINK QUESTIONS
CA-CCSS: CA.RL.9-10.1, CA.RL.9-10.3, CA.RL.9-10.2, CA.RL.9-10.4; CA.L.9-10.4a, CA.L.9-10.4c

1. What feelings do you think Luis expresses when he stands on top of the hubcaps and yells, "Someday, son, all this will be yours"? Use examples from the text and your own inferences to support your answer.

2. What personal qualities does Mr. Cintrón value, based on details in the text about his attitude and behavior? What does this teach readers about his character? Use examples from the text and your own inferences to support your answer.

3. What do you think is the significance of the title "Catch the Moon"? Use examples from the text and your inferences to support your answer.

4. Use the context to determine the meaning of the word **vulgar** as it is used in *Catch the Moon*. Write your definition of "vulgar" here and explain how you arrived at it.

5. Use context to determine the meaning of the word **dismantled** as it is used in *Catch the Moon*. Write your definition of "dismantled" here and show how you found it. Then, give a synonym for the word.

Please note that excerpts and passages in the StudySync® library and this workbook are intended as touchstones to generate interest in an author's work. The excerpts and passages do not substitute for the reading of entire texts, and StudySync® strongly recommends that students seek out and purchase the whole literary or informational work in order to experience it as the author intended. Links to online resellers are available in our digital library. In addition, complete works may be ordered through an authorized reseller by filling out and returning to StudySync® the order form enclosed in this workbook.

Reading & Writing Companion **63**

CLOSE READ
CA-CCSS: CA.RL.9-10.1, CA.RL.9-10.3, CA.RL.9-10.10, CA.RL.9-10.2, CA.W.9-10.2a, CA.W.9-10.2b, CA.W.9-10.4, CA.W.9-10.5, CA.W.9-10.6, CA.W.9-10.9a, CA.W.9-10.10

Reread the short story "Catch the Moon." As you reread, complete the Focus Questions below. Then use your answers and annotations from the questions to help you complete the Writing Prompt.

FOCUS QUESTIONS

1. What feelings and desires motivate Luis to organize and participate in the activities of the Tiburones, according to the first six paragraphs of the text?

2. Describe Luis's attitude toward and interactions with his father throughout the text and what these reveal about his character. Make annotations to explain your answer.

3. How does Luis's mother's death influence his behavior and emotions in different ways in the story? Highlight examples and make annotations to explain their significance.

4. What is the meaning of the title "Catch the Moon"? How does this relate to a theme of the story, according to evidence from the final two paragraphs of the text?

5. Throughout the story, how do Luis's interactions with Naomi serve to define his character?

WRITING PROMPT

How does Luis develop over the course of the story through his interaction with other characters? What do these interactions reveal about the theme of the story? Write a response to these questions. Cite evidence from the text to support your response.

AN AMERICAN CHILDHOOD

NON-FICTION

Annie Dillard
1987

INTRODUCTION

Annie Dillard described this book as "a memoir about parents, the world of science, and consciousness." In this excerpt, she uses the sensory details of a typical childhood morning to show how people develop a sense of awareness about themselves and the world.

"It drives you to a life of concentration, it does..."

NOTES

FIRST READ

Excerpt from Part One

1   The story starts back in 1950, when I was five.

2   Oh, the great humming silence of the empty neighborhoods in those days, the neighborhoods abandoned everywhere across continental America—the city residential areas, the new "suburbs," the towns and villages on the peopled highways, the cities, towns, and villages on the rivers, the shores, in the Rocky and Appalachian mountains, the **piedmont,** the dells, the bayous, the hills, the Great Basin, the Great Valley, the Great Plains—oh, the silence!

3   For every morning the neighborhoods emptied, and all vital activity, it seemed, set forth for parts unknown.

4   The men left in a rush: they flung on coats, they slid kisses at everybody's cheeks, they slammed house doors, they slammed car doors; they ground their cars' starters till the motors caught with a jump.

5   And the Catholic schoolchildren left in a rush. I saw them from our dining-room windows. They burst into the street buttoning their jackets; they threw dry catalpa pods at the stop sign and at each other. They hugged their brown-and-tan workbooks to them, clumped and parted, and proceeded toward St. Bede's church school almost by accident.

6   The men in their oval, empty cars drove slowly among the schoolchildren. The boys banged the cars' fenders with their hands, with their jackets' elbows, or their books. The men in cars inched among the children; they edged around corners and vanished from sight. The waving knots of children zigzagged and hollered up the street and vanished from sight. And inside all the forgotten houses in all the abandoned neighborhoods, the day of silence and waiting had begun.

NOTES

7   The war was over. People wanted to settle down, apparently, and calmly blow their way out of years of rationing. They wanted to bake sugary cakes, burn gas, go to church together, get rich, and make babies.

8   I had been born at the end of April 1945, on the day Hitler died; Roosevelt had died eighteen days before. My father had been 4-F in the war, because of a collapsing lung—despite his repeated and **chagrined** efforts to enlist. Now— five years after V-J Day—he still went out one night a week as a volunteer to the Civil Air Patrol; he searched the Pittsburgh skies for new enemy bombers. By day he worked downtown for American Standard.

9   Every woman stayed alone in her house in those days, like a coin in a safe. Amy and I lived alone with our mother most of the day. Amy was three years younger than I. Mother and Amy and I went our separate ways in peace.

10 The men had driven away and the schoolchildren had paraded out of sight. Now a self-conscious and **stricken** silence overtook the neighborhood, overtook our white corner house and myself inside. "Am I living?" In the kitchen I watched the unselfconscious trees through the screen door, until the trees' autumn branches like fins waved away the silence. I forgot myself, and sank into dim and watery oblivion.

11 A car passed. Its rush and whine jolted me from my blankness. The sound faded again and I faded again down into my hushed brain until the icebox motor kicked on and prodded me away. "You are living," the icebox motor said. "It is morning, morning, here in the kitchen, and you are in it," the icebox motor said, or the dripping faucet said, or any of the hundred other noisy things that only children can't stop hearing. Cars started, leaves rubbed, trucks' brakes whistled, sparrows peeped. Whenever it rained, the rain spattered, dripped, and ran, for the entire length of the shower, for the entire length of days-long rains, until we children were almost insane from hearing it rain because we couldn't stop hearing it rain. "Rinso white!" cried the man on the radio. "Rinso blue." The silence, like all silences, was made **poignant** and distinct by its sounds.

12 What a marvel it was that the day so often introduced itself with a firm footfall nearby. What a marvel it was that so many times a day the world, like a church bell, reminded me to recall and **contemplate** the durable fact that I was here, and had awakened once more to find myself set down in a going world.

13 In the living room the mail slot clicked open and envelopes clattered down. In the back room, where our maid, Margaret Butler, was ironing, the steam iron thumped the muffled ironing board and hissed. The walls squeaked, the pipes knocked, the screen door trembled, the furnace banged, and the radiators clanged. This was the fall the loud trucks went by. I sat mindless and eternal on the kitchen floor, stony of head and solemn, playing with my fingers.

Copyright © BookheadEd Learning, LLC

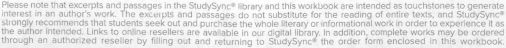

Time streamed in full flood beside me on the kitchen floor; time roared raging beside me down its swollen banks; and when I woke I was so startled I fell in.

14 Who could ever tire of this heart-stopping transition, of this breakthrough shift between seeing and knowing you see, between being and knowing you be? It drives you to a life of concentration, it does, a life in which effort draws you down so very deep that when you surface you twist up **exhilarated** with a yelp and a gasp.

15 Who could ever tire of this radiant transition, this surfacing to awareness and this deliberate plunging to oblivion—the theater curtain rising and falling? Who could tire of it when the sum of those moments at the edge—the conscious life we so dread losing—is all we have, the gift at the moment of opening it?

Excerpted from An American Childhood *by Annie Dillard, published by Harper & Row.*

THINK QUESTIONS CA-CCSS: CA.RI.9-10.1, CA.RI.9-10.4, CA.L.9-10.4a, CA.L.9-10.4d, CA.RL.9-10.4

1. What do details about five-year-old Annie's neighborhood and home suggest about her family, including their social class? Use details from the text to support your answer.

2. Why is the Dillards' house so silent? How does Annie feel about this silence? Support your answer with figurative language from the text.

3. What are some of the sounds that Annie hears while she plays in the kitchen? What effect do these sounds have on her? Why do you think she personifies these sounds? What other examples of figurative language does she use? Cite evidence from the text to support your answer.

4. Remembering that the Latin root *ped* means "foot" and that the Latin root *mons* means "mountain," use context clues to determine the meaning of the word **piedmont** as it is used in paragraph 2 of *An American Childhood*. Write your definition of "piedmont" and explain how you determined its meaning. Then confirm your inferred meaning in a print or digital dictionary, revising your definition, if needed.

5. Use the context clues provided in the text to determine the meaning of **chagrined** as it is used in paragraph 8 of *An American Childhood*. Write your definition of "chagrined" and explain how you determined its meaning. Then check a print or digital dictionary to find the precise meaning of the word and its pronunciation.

CLOSE READ

CA-CCSS: CA.RI.9-10.1, CA.RI.9-10.2, CA.RI.9-10.3, CA.RI.9-10.4, CA.RI.9-10.6, CA.L.9-10.5a, CA.W.9-10.2b, CA.W.9-10.3a, CA.W.9-10.3c, CA.W.9-10.3d, CA.W.9-10.3e, CA.W.9-10.4, CA.W.9-10.5, CA.W.9-10.6, CA.W.9-10.9b, CA.W.9-10.10

Reread the excerpt from *An American Childhood*. As you reread, complete the Focus Questions below. Then use your answers and annotations from the questions to help you complete the Writing Prompt.

FOCUS QUESTIONS

1. What purpose do paragraphs 1–9 of this excerpt from Dillard's memoir serve? Analyze their significance in terms of the excerpt as a whole.

2. In paragraph 10, Annie asks herself "'Am I living?'" What answer does she arrive at, and how does she find it? What figurative language and imagery does she use to convey the central (or main) idea of the excerpt?

3. Where and how is the central idea of the text first introduced? How does Dillard use personification to develop, shape, and refine the central idea of the excerpt?

4. Paragraphs 13–15 contain an extended metaphor about Time. Identify and explain the comparison Dillard makes. What central idea in the text does the author express through this metaphor? How does understanding the metaphor enrich your understanding of the excerpt as a whole?

5. What impression do you have of five-year-old Annie's character? How do her interactions with other people, with objects and sounds inside and outside the house, and with her own thoughts define her? How does the writer Annie Dillard's use of and interaction with language, including figurative language, help to define the younger Annie's character and ideas?

WRITING PROMPT

Annie Dillard demonstrates a keen awareness of sounds, finding deeper meaning in them, in her memoir *An American Childhood*. Now it's your turn. Using the memoir as a model, write a personal narrative about a time when you were deeply moved by a sensory experience. Perhaps you were at a concert and were affected by the sounds you heard. Perhaps you were on a nature walk and saw or smelled a field of flowers you will never forget. Describe the sensory experience through the use of descriptive details and figurative language, and explain why it has a special meaning to you. What was the situation? Who was involved? What insight or revelation did it leave you with? Use the first-person ("I") point of view to tell your true story. Also, use narrative details to develop the experience and to sequence the events. Use quotations from the memoir to support your idea and to compare Dillard's experience to your own. Provide a strong introduction and a conclusion that reflects on what you learned from the experience.

Please note that excerpts and passages in the StudySync® library and this workbook are intended as touchstones to generate interest in an author's work. The excerpts and passages do not substitute for the reading of entire texts, and StudySync® strongly recommends that students seek out and purchase the whole literary or informational work in order to experience it as the author intended. Links to online resellers are available in our digital library. In addition, complete works may be ordered through an authorized reseller by filling out and returning to StudySync® the order form enclosed in this workbook.

Reading & Writing Companion 69

THOSE WINTER SUNDAYS

POETRY
Robert Hayden
1966

INTRODUCTION

studysync tv

obert Hayden was a 20th century African-American poet and essayist. Ostracized by his peers and stressed by a tumultuous home environment, Hayden turned to books at a young age. His early literary skills stayed with him, and in time Hayden was able to earn a living through the written word. His poems often balance painful experiences with hope, possibility, and a celebration of humanity. In "Those Winter Sundays," the speaker reminisces about his father.

"What did I know, what did I know…?"

 FIRST READ

NOTES

1 Sundays too my father got up early
2 and put his clothes on in the **blueblack** cold,
3 then with cracked hands that ached
4 from labor in the weekday weather made
5 banked fires blaze. No one ever thanked him.
6 I'd wake and hear the cold **splintering,** breaking.
7 When the rooms were warm, he'd call,
8 and slowly I would rise and dress,
9 fearing the **chronic** angers of that house,
10 Speaking **indifferently** to him,
11 who had driven out the cold
12 and polished my good shoes as well.
13 What did I know, what did I know
14 of love's **austere** and lonely offices?

"Those Winter Sundays". Copyright © 1966 by Robert Hayden, from COLLECTED POEMS
OF ROBERT HAYDEN by Robert Hayden, edited by Frederick Glaysher. Copyright ©
1985 by Emma Hayden. Used by permission of Liveright Publishing Corporation.

 THINK QUESTIONS   CA-CCSS: CA.RL.9-10.1, CA.RL.9-10.4, CA.L.9-10.4a, CA.L.9-10.4b

1. Who is the speaker of the poem? Cite evidence from the text to support your answer.

2. Use details from the text to write two or three sentences describing the way the speaker treated the father in the past.

3. Write two or three sentences explaining the physical and emotional living conditions in the family. Support your answer with textual evidence.

4. Use context to determine the meaning of the word **indifferently** as it is used in "Those Winter Sundays". Write your definition of "indifferently" here and tell how you found it. What part of speech is "indifferently," and how do you know? What is its base word? Using a dictionary if necessary, list some other forms of this word, and explain how the meaning changes.

5. Remembering that the Greek root "*chron*" means "time" and the suffix "*ic*" means "related to," use the context clues provided in the passage to determine the meaning of **chronic**. Write your definition of "chronic" here and tell how you got it.

CLOSE READ

CA-CCSS: CA.RL.9-10.1, CA.RL.9-10.2, CA.RL.9-10.3, CA.RL.9-10.4, CA.L.9-10.4a, CA.W.9-10.2b, CA.W.9-10.4, CA.W.9-10.5

Reread the poem "Those Winter Sundays." As you reread, complete the Focus Questions below. Then use your answers and annotations from the questions to help you complete the Writing Prompt.

FOCUS QUESTIONS

1. How would you describe the character of the father? Write a brief description. Cite details from the poem that support your description, and make annotations to explain your choices.

2. Reread lines 1 and 2. How would you describe the tone of these lines? Does the tone express a simple attitude or a complex one? Which words and phrases have strong connotations that add to this tone? Support your answer with textual evidence and make annotations to explain your answer choices.

3. Reread lines 6–9 and identify an example of figurative language in these lines. What things are being compared? How do the connotations of words in this comparison help to make it stronger? Highlight textual evidence and make annotations to explain your ideas.

4. Reread the final line. What does the speaker understand as an adult that he did not understand as a child? In what way is the tone of this line different from the rest of the poem? What words, phrases, or other poetic techniques create or affect this tone? Support your response with evidence from the text.

5. How would you restate the theme of this poem? Highlight evidence from the text and use annotations to support your answer.

WRITING PROMPT

The Essential Question for this unit is, "How do our interactions define us?" In a short essay, describe how the speaker's interactions with his father as a youth define him as an adult. What important lessons did his upbringing ultimately teach him? How does the tone of the poem help to support these ideas? Include details about how the poet's choice of words with strong connotations, figurative language, and techniques such as sound devices help to create the tone.

THE CHRISTMAS TRUCE OF 1914

English Language
Development

NON-FICTION

INTRODUCTION

World War I was a disastrous war, full of unimaginable agony among the troops. However, early in the war, a remarkable truce occurred. What was it that made enemy troops, for a short while, stop fighting and become friends?

"Soldiers began to celebrate the holiday."

 FIRST READ

 NOTES

1 Every war is a terrible event. World War I was one of the most dreadful. It lasted from 1914 to 1918. More than 25 million people were killed or wounded. At first, people were certain that the war would end quickly. Fighting would be over by Christmas. It was not. The war had come to a bloody standstill by the end of the first year. Soldiers would not be home for a long, long time.

2 Part of the war was waged in Europe. It was called the Western Front. A long line of battlefields stretched across Europe. Battles were fought from Belgium down through France. Conditions were brutal. The soldiers lived in horrendous **trenches**. An area called "no man's land" separated them. The enemy trenches in some places were close. Soldiers could hear the enemy talking with each other.

3 November of the first year came. The war had been on for three months. English and German soldiers were already exhausted. Soldiers in some areas adopted a "live and let live" attitude. Sometimes they **tacitly** agreed to stop shooting. They could then claim their casualties from no man's land. And they could bury their dead. Occasionally, the men would **banter** back and forth. Some claim that this led to the Christmas **truce** of 1914.

4 The weather in December of 1914 had been miserable. Constant rain soaked everything. Mud was everywhere. Life was very unpleasant. On Christmas Eve, a hard frost set in. Snow dusted the ground. Perhaps it was this sudden change in weather. Perhaps it was the Christmas season. Somehow war stopped along parts of the Western Front. Soldiers began to celebrate the holiday.

5 German soldiers lit candles. They put small trees along the trench border. Then something magical happened. The Germans began to sing a Christmas carol. The British soldiers responded with one of theirs. Then they joined together to sing "O Come, All Ye Faithful." The British sang in English, and the

Reading & Writing Companion

NOTES

Germans sang in Latin. Singing was heard on both sides in different places.

6   On Christmas morning, men slowly emerged from the trenches. They were going to greet the enemy. They were cautious, of course. But no one fired any shots. Men shouted Christmas greetings instead. They exchanged gifts. They took photos. A German soldier cut the hair of a British soldier. The German had once been a barber. In some places, the men played soccer.

7   Some diaries and letters have survived. They tell of many exchanges among the enemies. The men on opposite sides did in fact stop fighting. They socialized instead. There are only estimates of the number of troops involved. Some say about 100,000 people participated. If the men had been left to themselves, the war would have likely ended. The idea is summed up in the words of a German soldier: "We are Saxons. You are Anglo-Saxons. What is there to fight about?"

8   In some areas, the truce continued for nearly a week. Eventually it ended. The British High Command called associating with the enemy "treason." Officers were not to allow soldiers to be friendly. The truce was not official. It could not be allowed. It was illegal. High Command feared that the socializing might continue. That could lead to **mutiny**. It could end the war. It was declared that anyone befriending the enemy would be harshly punished. Commanding officers clearly wanted the war to continue. A German Corporal named Adolf Hitler explained, "Such a thing should not happen in wartime. Have you no German sense of honor?"

9   The men on both sides shared brutal experiences. They could understand each other's pain. They might even have been friends under different circumstances. The Christmas truce was a moment of light in a horrible war.

10 The war continued. Fighting became more savage. Sadly, the truce was never repeated.

⚙ USING LANGUAGE   CA-CCSS: ELD.PI.9-10.6.c.Ex

Read each sentence. Choose the correct meaning of the boldfaced word in each given sentence. You can refer to the table below for a list of the meanings of common prefixes and suffixes.

Prefixes		Suffixes	
un-: not; opposite	*pre-*: before	*-able*: fit for; tending to	*-ment*: condition of
over-: too much	*en-*: cause to	*-dom*: place or state of being	*-ize*: to make; to become

1. Many of the soldiers were **unhappy** until the truce happened.

    ○ very happy
    ○ not happy

2. The trenches were so close the soldiers could see each other **breathing**.

    ○ not continue to breathe
    ○ continue to breathe

3. The soldier woke up only to realize he had **overslept**.

    ○ slept too much
    ○ caused to sleep

4. Is there any way you could **preview** this speech ahead of tonight's event?

    ○ view before
    ○ view too much

5. The trenches were not a **comfortable** place to live.

    ○ fit for comfort
    ○ before comfort

6. There was an **argument** last night about how to help the team raise money.

    ○ condition of arguing
    ○ one who argues

7. Try to **enjoy** the day despite the drizzling rain.

    ○ not feel joy
    ○ cause to feel joy

8. I hope to **categorize** all the data by the end of the day.

    ○ condition of categories
    ○ make categories

👥 MEANINGFUL INTERACTIONS CA-CCSS: ELD.PI.9-10.1.Ex, ELD.PI.9-10.6.a.Ex

How does the author support main ideas in the text? Focus your discussion on paragraphs 6 and 7. Review the boldfaced text. You can use the speaking frames below to help express your ideas in the discussion. Remember to follow turn-taking rules during the discussion. Then, use the self-assessment rubric to evaluate your participation in the discussion.

6 On Christmas morning, men slowly emerged from the trenches. They were going to greet the enemy. They were cautious, of course. But no one fired any shots. Men shouted Christmas greetings instead. **They exchanged gifts. They took photos. A German soldier cut the hair of a British soldier. The German had once been a barber.** In some places, the men played soccer.

7 **Some diaries and letters have survived.** They tell of many exchanges among the enemies. **The men on opposite sides did in fact stop fighting.** They socialized instead. There are only estimates of the number of troops involved. Some say about 100,000 people participated. If the men had been left to themselves, the war would have likely ended. **The idea is summed up in the words of a German soldier: "We are Saxons. You are Anglo-Saxons. What is there to fight about?"**

- I think that the use of . . . effectively supports the main ideas in the text because . . .

- The author explains that . . . exist from that time, and they tell us that . . .

- The direct quote from the German soldier helps to show . . .

- As a result, the author is able to . . . effectively, and this helps the reader . . .

- Another main idea in the text is . . . It is supported by . . .

- I think . . . , what do you think about . . . ?

- I really like what . . . said, and I would like to add . . .

⚙ SELF-ASSESSMENT RUBRIC CA-CCSS: ELD.PI.9-10.1.Ex, ELD.PI.9-10.6.a.Ex

	4 I did this well.	3 I did this pretty well	2 I did this a little bit.	1 I did not do this.
I expressed my Ideas clearly.				
I supported my ideas using evidence from the text.				
I explained how the author supports the main ideas in the text.				
I took turns sharing my opinions with the group.				

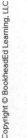

REREAD

Reread paragraphs 1–5 of "The Christmas Truce of 1914." After you reread, complete the Using Language and Meaningful Interactions activities.

USING LANGUAGE   CA-CCSS: ELD.PII.9-10.3.Ex

Write the correct tense of the verb in the blank for each sentence below.

1.   Write the correct **past** tense of the verb "die" in the following sentence:

   Millions of men _____ in World War I.

2.   Write the correct **future** tense of the verb "learn" in the following sentence:

   Future generations _____ about the "Christmas Truce."

3.   Write the correct **simple present** form of the verb "run" in the following sentence:

   The soldiers _____ every morning at six.

4.   Write the correct **past progressive** form of the verb "writing" in the following sentence:

   The soldier _____ a letter home.

5.   Write the correct **perfect past** form of the verb "clean" in the following sentence:

   The cook _____ the pots before lunch began.

MEANINGFUL INTERACTIONS CA-CCSS: ELD.PI.9-10.1.Ex, ELD.PI.9-10.6.b.Ex

The author says, "Every war is a terrible event." The author then says that World War I was one of the worst wars. Discuss: Why is war terrible? What made World War I a "dreadful" war? Why was the "Christmas Truce" so special? Do you think the war might have ended if it was up to the soldiers? Why or why not? Remember to ask questions that are relevant and on-topic. Then, use the self-assessment rubric to evaluate your participation in the discussion.

- I think war is / is not terrible because . . .

- World War I was a "dreadful" war because . . .

- Evidence from the text suggests . . .

- Do you think that . . . ?

- What do you think about the "Christmas Truce"?

- Your comment indicates that . . .

- As a result of the discussion, I think . . .

SELF-ASSESSMENT RUBRIC CA-CCSS: ELD.PI.9-10.1.Ex, ELD.PI.9 10.6.b.Ex

	4 I did this well.	3 I did this pretty well.	2 I did this a little bit.	1 I did not do this.
I expressed my ideas clearly.				
I supported my ideas using evidence from the text.				
I used the text to make inferences and conclusions.				
I asked and answered relevant, on-topic questions.				

 REREAD

Reread paragraphs 6–10 of "The Christmas Truce of 1914." After you reread, complete the Using Language and Meaningful Interactions activities.

USING LANGUAGE CA-CCSS: ELD.PII.9-10.4.Ex

Fill in each blank to create an expanded noun phrase for each sentence.

1. Write an expanded noun phrase for "soldiers" in the following sentence.

    _____ soldiers exchanged gifts.

2. Write an expanded noun phrase for "gifts" that tells what kind of gifts in the following sentence.

    The soldiers exchanged _____ gifts.

3. Write an expanded noun phrase for "fighting" that tells where the fighting is in the following sentence.

    The fighting _____ became more savage.

4. Write an expanded noun phrase for "hair" that tells whose hair it is in the following sentence.

    A German soldier even cut the hair _____.

5. Write an expanded noun phrase for "officers" that tells which officers in the following sentence.

    Officers _____ worried that the socializing would continue.

MEANINGFUL INTERACTIONS CA-CCSS: ELD.PI.9-10.1.Ex, ELD.PI.9-10.6.a.Ex, ELD.PI.9-10.7.Ex

Discuss these questions: How does the author structure the text? How does the text structure help the author provide evidence for key details? What are some key details the author provides? You can use the speaking frames below to help express your ideas in the discussion.

- I think the text structure the author uses is . . .

- An example of that text structure is . . .

- Another text structure the author uses is . . .

- An example of that text structure is . . .

- Two key details the author provides are . . .

- I know these details are important because . . .

WHEN EVERYTHING CHANGED

English Language
Development

POETRY

INTRODUCTION

n this poem, a new student comes to school. She is different from her classmates, and sits alone. Then, a classmate decides to approach her. Could this decision change both of their lives forever?

"And I knew what they were thinking, And I did not care."

 FIRST READ

1 My mother used to tell me

2 Things happen for a reason.

3 When I was in high school,

4 I learned she was right.

5 "Class," Ms. Derry said,

6 "meet Bianca Caprelli, a new student.

7 Her family just moved here from Italy."

8 After her announcement,

9 We all stared at this girl.

10 This outsider.

11 Her clothes,

12 Not our usual uniform of jeans, sassy shirt, sneakers.

13 Everything matched: shoes, shirt, pants, even her purse.

14 When she spoke, her words sang,

15 Almost like a familiar but forgotten **melody**.

16 She didn't belong in our closed world full of giggles,

17 Mockery,

18 Football games,

19 **Proms**.

20 Our tight world belonged to us.

21 We were important,

22 **Esteemed**, and

23 Revered.

24 At lunch, she sat alone,

25 Looking like a frightened deer.

26 The others laughed and pointed.

27 They **ridiculed** her clothes.

28 They imitated her accent.

29 They giggled and sneered.

30 Their sneering snaked across the room

31 And shattered her.

32 And I . . . I felt sorry for her.

33 On pizza day, at lunch,

34 I sat down next to her,

35 Breaking the rules of the Others.

36 They glared at me.

37 "Hi," I said, feeling their sword stares,

38 "I'm Anna. Can I sit with you?"

39 Her smile was shy,

40 Likable.

41 She missed Italy and riding her bike in the city.

42 I asked if she wanted a tour of the town after school.

43 She nodded as a smile lit her face.

44 The Others left together,

45 ignoring us.

46 And I knew what they were thinking,

47 And I did not care.

48 That day in the lunchroom was long ago.

49 This afternoon my best friend and I will take our children

50 To volunteer at the animal **shelter**.

51 "Because," Bianca says, "they must learn that all of us need a friend."

52 A lesson I hope they will learn.

⚙ USING LANGUAGE CA-CCSS: ELD.PII.9-10.3.Ex

Complete the sentences by choosing the correct verb tense.

1. As we discuss the poem, we discover that the text _____ a friendship.

   ○ is describing   ○ was describing

2. The girl _____ at the front of the classroom when the teacher introduced her.

   ○ is standing   ○ was standing

3. Anna and the other girls _____ at her clothes, which all matched.

   ○ are staring   ○ were staring

4. Bianca _____ alone as Anna came over to her table.

   ○ is sitting   ○ was sitting

5. As the girls _____, they learned a lot about each other.

   ○ are talking   ○ were talking

6. The Others _____ them as the girls left together.

   ○ are ignoring   ○ were ignoring

7. It is not a school day, so Bianca and Anna _____ their children to the animal shelter.

   ○ are taking   ○ were taking

8. While I _____ the poem, I think about how it relates to my own life.

   ○ am reading   ○ was reading

👥 MEANINGFUL INTERACTIONS CA-CCSS: ELD.PI.9-10.1.Ex, ELD.PI.9-10.6.b.Ex

What does the poem "When Everything Changed" reveal about the characters of Anna and Bianca? Consider the boldfaced text as you make inferences and draw conclusions. You can use the speaking frames below the text to help express your ideas in the discussion. Remember to affirm others' ideas during the discussion. Then, use the self-assessment rubric to evaluate your participation in the discussion.

8 After her announcement,

9 We all stared at this girl.

10 This outsider.

11 **Her clothes,**

12 **Not our usual uniform of jeans, sassy shirt, sneakers.**

13 **Everything matched: shoes, shirt, pants, even her purse.**

14 **When she spoke, her words sang,**

15 Almost like a familiar but forgotten melody.

24 At lunch, **she sat alone,**

25 **Looking like a frightened deer.**

26 The others laughed and pointed.

27 They ridiculed her clothes,

28 They imitated her accent.

29 They giggled and sneered.

30 **Their sneering snaked across the room**

31 **and shattered her.**

32 And I . . . **I felt sorry for her.**

33 On pizza day, at lunch,

34 **I sat down next to her,**

35 **Breaking the rules of the Others.**

36 They glared at me.

- The poem suggests Anna is someone who . . . and Bianca is someone who . . .
- One way the poet describes Anna in line . . . is with the word(s) . . .
- These words or phrases make me think Anna is a . . . person because . . .
- The text creates the impression that Bianca feels . . . because . . .
- What do you think about . . . ?
- I really like what . . . said, and as a result, I would like to add . . .

 ## SELF-ASSESSMENT RUBRIC CA-CCSS: ELD.PI.9-10.1.Ex, ELD.PI.9-10.6.b.Ex

	4 I did this well.	3 I did this pretty well.	2 I did this a little bit.	1 I did not do this.
I made inferences and drew conclusions about the characters of Anna and Bianca based on details in the text.				
I expressed my ideas clearly using appropriate verb tenses.				
I supported my ideas using evidence from the text.				
I affirmed the ideas and opinions of other students in the group.				

REREAD

Reread lines 1–32 of "When Everything Changed." After you reread, complete the Using Language and Meaningful Interactions activities.

USING LANGUAGE CA-CCSS: ELD.PII.9-10.1.Ex

Complete the sentences by filling in the blanks.

1. **How many stanzas are in this reading?**

   This reading has _____ stanzas.

2. **How many lines are in the first stanza?**

   There are _____ lines.

3. **What is the second stanza about?**

   The second stanza is about _____.

4. **What simile does the author include in the third stanza?**

   In the third stanza, the author includes _____.

5. **What image does the language in the fourth stanza create?**

   Language in the fourth stanza creates _____.

6. **What scene does the author describe in the fifth stanza?**

   In the fifth stanza, the author describes _____.

7. **What metaphor does the author use in the fifth stanza to describe the effect of the girls' sneering?**

   In the fifth stanza, the author describes how _____
   _____.

8. **Which stanzas make up the flashback in the poem?**

   The stanzas _____.

MEANINGFUL INTERACTIONS CA-CCSS: ELD.PI.9-10.1.Ex, ELD.PI.9-10.6.a.Ex

The author of "When Everything Changed" structures the plot of the narrative poem through cause-and-effect relationships. Review lines 8 to 32 from the poem. Then identify the cause-and-effect relationships. Use the speaking frames to help express your ideas. Remember to ask and answer relevant, on-topic questions during your discussion. Then, use the self-assessment rubric to evaluate your participation in the discussion.

- Bianca seems like an outsider to the other girls because . . .

- Bianca is not part of Anna's group because . . .

- The girls laugh at Bianca at lunch because . . .

- Their laughter causes Bianca to . . .

- I know this because the text says that . . .

- Their laughter causes Anna to . . .

- One reason the poet might use a cause-and-effect text structure is . . .

SELF-ASSESSMENT RUBRIC CA-CCSS: ELD.PI.9-10.1.Ex, ELD.PI.9-10.6.a.Ex

	4 I did this well.	3 I did this pretty well.	2 I did this a little bit.	1 I did not do this.
I explained how the writer used cause-and-effect relationships in the text.				
I expressed my ideas clearly.				
I supported my ideas using evidence from the text.				
I asked or answered questions that were relevant to the topic.				

REREAD

Reread lines 33–52 of "When Everything Changed." After you reread, complete the Using Language and Meaningful Interactions activities.

⚙ USING LANGUAGE CA-CCSS: ELD.PII.9-10.2.a.Ex

Read each line from the poem and study the boldfaced word or words. Then identify another line from the text that contains a word or words that refer back to the boldfaced text.

1. "Class," Ms. Derry said, "meet **Bianca Caprelli**, a new student." (lines 5–6)

    ○ "Her family moved here from Italy."
    ○ Almost like a familiar but forgotten melody.

2. We were **important,** (line 21)

    ○ Esteemed, and Revered.
    ○ At lunch, she sat alone,

3. **The others** laughed and pointed. (line 26)

    ○ Everything matched: shoes, shirt, pants, even her purse.
    ○ They ridiculed her clothes.

4. They imitated her accent. They giggled and **sneered**. (lines 28–29)

    ○ Their sneering snaked across the room,
    ○ And I . . . I felt sorry for her.

5. **The Others** left together, ignoring us. (lines 44–45)

    ○ And I knew what they were thinking
    ○ And I did not care.

Reading & Writing Companion

👥 MEANINGFUL INTERACTIONS CA-CCSS: ELD.PI.9-10.3.Ex

Answer this question based on what you have read in "When Everything Changed." Do we help others the most through our personal interactions, or are different solutions needed for situations such as the one presented in the poem? Use the speaking frames below to help you express your point of view and persuade others to agree.

- My opinion is that personal interactions are most helpful to resolve these kinds of situations because . . .

OR

- My opinion is that different solutions are required to resolve these kinds of situations because . . .

- One reason why I believe this is . . .

- The text supports my point of view because . . .

- Would you say that again? I think you said . . .

- Why do you think that? Do you think . . . ?

- That is an interesting idea. However, I believe . . .

- I see your point, but . . .

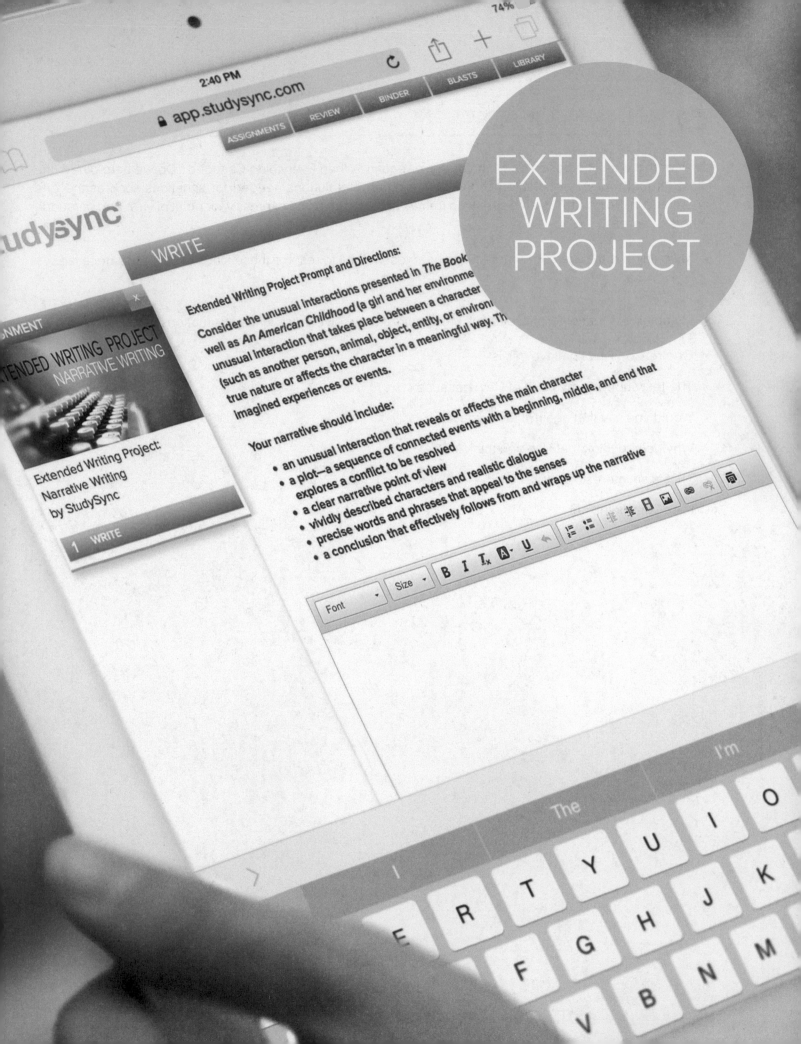

EXTENDED WRITING PROJECT

WRITE

Extended Writing Project Prompt and Directions:

Consider the unusual interactions presented in *The Book*
well as *An American Childhood* (a girl and her environme
unusual interaction that takes place between a character
(such as another person, animal, object, entity, or environ
true nature or affects the character in a meaningful way. Th
imagined experiences or events.

Your narrative should include:

- an unusual interaction that reveals or affects the main character
- a plot—a sequence of connected events with a beginning, middle, and end that explores a conflict to be resolved
- a clear narrative point of view
- vividly described characters and realistic dialogue
- precise words and phrases that appeal to the senses
- a conclusion that effectively follows from and wraps up the narrative

---

EXTENDED WRITING PROJECT
NARRATIVE WRITING

Extended Writing Project:
Narrative Writing
by StudySync

1 WRITE

NARRATIVE WRITING

WRITING PROMPT

Consider the unusual interactions presented in *The Book Thief* (Death and a survivor) as well as *An American Childhood* (a girl and her environment). Write a narrative about an unusual interaction that takes place between a character and someone or something else (such as another person, animal, object, entity, or environment) that reveals the character's true nature or affects the character in a meaningful way. The narrative may reflect real or imagined experiences or events.

Your narrative should include:

- an unusual interaction that reveals or affects the main character
- a plot—a sequence of connected events with a beginning, middle, and end that explores a conflict to be resolved
- a clear narrative point of view
- vividly described characters and realistic dialogue
- precise words and phrases that appeal to the senses
- a conclusion that effectively follows from and wraps up the narrative

Narrative writing tells a story of real or imagined experiences or events. Narratives can be fiction, such as stories and poems, or non-fiction, such as memoirs and personal essays. Good narrative writing uses effective techniques, relevant descriptive details, vivid language, and well-structured event sequences to convey a story to readers. The features of narrative writing include:

- a beginning that establishes a narrative point of view and introduces the characters and setting

- a plot that revolves around a conflict or problem to be solved
- transitions that indicate a clear sequence of events
- techniques such as dialogue and pacing to develop the experiences, events, and characters
- precise, descriptive language and sensory details
- a conclusion that follows from the rest of the narrative and points to a theme, or message

As you continue with this extended writing project, you will receive more instruction and practice crafting each of the elements of narrative writing to create your own compelling narrative.

 ## STUDENT MODEL

Before you get started on your own narrative about an interaction, read this narrative that one student wrote in response to the writing prompt. As you read the model, highlight and annotate the features of narrative writing that this student included in her story.

Kelsey and the Poet

Kelsey was sitting on the lawn, watching the movers carry boxes out of her house, when Sharif, the mail carrier, walked up to the house at his usual time, wearing a summer uniform of blue shorts and a pale gray safari helmet.

"Sneaking out in broad daylight?" he said, smiling, as he handed her a sheaf of envelopes.

"Didn't we tell you we're moving?" she said with dismay. "I know Dad sent in a forwarding address." She began leafing through the envelopes in her hand. "I guess we'll get just as much junk mail in Oregon as in Utah, won't we?" Then she took in a sudden gasping breath, for at the sight of the return address on a greeting-card-size envelope, she became too stunned to utter words. "It's from a magazine I sent one of my poems to."

She hastily tore open the envelope and saw a two-line note with one line of handwriting under it. Under that there was a second page. The second page was a dozen short lines in big italics.

"Oh, no!" she cried out.

"They sent it back," Sharif said, understandingly.

"This is terrible. I'll never get anything published."

Sharif read Kelsey's poem over her shoulder. "May I? 'First Feelings.' I like that title. How old are you?"

"Fifteen, and this is the first manuscript I've ever sent anywhere, and I'm already a miserable failure! This is a terrible omen! I'm never going to do anything worthwhile! I'm doomed for life!"

Kelsey remembered how excited she'd been when she first mailed the poem to the magazine. She'd been positive that all she had to do was wait a couple of weeks and there'd be an answering letter—no, a thrilled, thrilling phone call—telling her that the magazine was honored to have discovered America's newest literary talent. She'd bought herself an ice cream sundae just to celebrate mailing the stupid thing!

Being fifteen is a total embarrassment, Kelsey thought, *especially when you're not a published poet yet.* She gritted her teeth at the futility of her efforts.

"I think I was seventeen when I got my first rejection," Sharif said. "I had a similar attitude, if I remember correctly."

She gave him a look of surprise. "Are you a poet too?"

"I sure am." Without warning he poured forth words about someone taking a long walk. They were beautiful, sorrowful, silken, somehow violet-colored words about not knowing what to do. They might have been written just for her.

"How can you be a poet," she asked, "when you're a mailman?"

He laughed heartily. "I write in my head as I walk my route."

Kelsey was trying to visualize herself in a safari helmet, treading along on a suburban sidewalk in solitude, but after a couple of seconds the scene of her fantasy changed to a steaming, overgrown jungle like in an old movie, where she was hacking away at the underbrush, with the howling of monkeys in the background. Then she was back in the real world—just a girl who'd gotten bad news, moaning to someone she didn't really know well.

Please note that excerpts and passages in the StudySync® library and this workbook are intended as touchstones to generate interest in an author's work. The excerpts and passages do not substitute for the reading of entire texts, and StudySync® strongly recommends that students seek out and purchase the whole literary or informational work in order to experience it as the author intended. Links to online resellers are available in our digital library. In addition, complete works may be ordered through an authorized reseller by filling out and returning to StudySync® the order form enclosed in this workbook.

Reading & Writing
Companion

93

"Have you ever published anything?" she asked Sharif.

"Now and then, in online magazines. They don't pay their writers, but their readers are primarily other poets, and so we write letters about each other's work, which makes it rewarding in other ways than money."

"Do you think you'll ever be famous?"

He laughed again, and told her that no, he probably never would be, except among a couple of hundred people—but, he added, they were people who really understood poetry.

"Well, if you'll excuse me," he said, "I have to keep going on my appointed rounds."

Kelsey glanced over her shoulder; the inside of the moving van was already half full of boxes.

"Thanks for being a great mailman," she said, shaking his hand. "And a great poet."

He shook his head, smiling to himself as if he knew something she didn't. Then he walked away.

As soon as she and her family were on the road in their little silver sedan, Kelsey began wishing she had a copy of Sharif's poem. But of course he wouldn't carry copies of his poems in his postal uniform, and even if she wanted to write to him for a copy, she didn't know his last name or address. Once they were settled in their new home, she confided in her mom about this, and Mom suggested mailing a letter to "Mail Carrier Sharif" at the zip code of their old Utah post office. The next day, Kelsey went to the nearest mailbox to send him a letter, and she envisioned herself receiving his reply and unfolding a poetic masterpiece.

She never got a reply from him, but she'd imagined it, and she knew that an active imagination was really important for a poet.

☁ THINK QUESTIONS

1. What is the main problem or conflict in this story? Refer to details from the text that present and develop it.

2. How does dialogue contribute to the plot and characterization in this story? Mention two or more lines of dialogue and specify what they contribute.

3. What is the crucial interaction in the story? What does it reveal about the main character? Refer to specific details from the interaction in your answer.

4. As you consider the writing prompt, which selections, Blasts, or other resources would you like to examine to help you create your own narrative?

5. Based on what you have read, listened to, or researched so far, how would you answer the question, *How do our interactions define us?*

SKILL: ORGANIZE NARRATIVE WRITING

⭐ DEFINE

A narrative is a story; it may be fictional or nonfictional. In either case, the basic elements of a narrative are **plot, character, setting,** and **theme.** An effective plot revolves around a **conflict,** or problem, the characters must face. It might be an **external conflict,** such as a conflict between the main character and another person or between the main character and the forces of nature. However, it might also be an **internal conflict,** or a character's struggle with something in his or her own nature, such as a debate about which of two careers to pursue. The opening part of the narrative, which introduces the setting, characters, and conflict, is called the **exposition.**

The plot develops through a **sequence of events,** each one related to the next. At times, the author may rearrange the order in which the events are narrated—such as in a **flashback,** a scene that returns to the past—but in almost all cases, the reader is able to figure out the chronological order in which the events occurred. The sequence builds to a **climax** or turning point, when the main character faces a crucial test in dealing with the problem.

Authors use a toolkit of literary techniques to tell their stories. Descriptive **details,** such as those about the setting or the characters' appearances, help readers participate imaginatively in the narrative. A key structural factor is **point of view,** or the perspective from which the story is told.

The **narrator** might be a character in the narrative (usually the main character), telling the tale in his or her own words in the **first person.** More often, the narrator is an unidentified voice telling the story from an outside perspective in the **third person,** using *he* or *she* for all the characters and *I* for none of them. The writer's choice of who will narrate the story affects what events and details the reader will have access to and how the reader will understand and react to the characters.

Characters are the driving force of a story. Many plots move forward through a series of **interactions** between characters, conveyed by action and **dialogue.** Characters often undergo a significant change by the story's end, and the change may be a strong indication of a **theme**—a main idea—that the author seeks to develop in the text. Themes are likely to be visible throughout a story, but especially at the **conclusion,** when the shape of the whole plot is complete, the main conflict is **resolved**—perhaps successfully for the main character or perhaps not—and the reader as well as the characters are left to remember and reflect on what has occurred.

IDENTIFICATION AND APPLICATION

- A story's narrator helps to orient readers with the details of the story, such as where and when the story takes place and who the story is about.

- Characters are the heart of a narrative. Their interactions show who they are and help move the plot forward. Characters develop and change in the course of a story.

- The plot is built upon a conflict that is interesting to readers—an important problem that the main character tries to solve. The conflict may be external (the character grapples with an outside force or another person) or internal (the character struggles with something in his or her own nature).

- Plot events are organized in a clear sequence, usually in chronological order.

- The sequence of events builds to a climax, the point at which characters are forced to take action, and finally a conclusion, in which the conflict is resolved.

- Techniques such as point of view and flashback, as well as vividly described details of setting, characters, and action, bring a narrative to life.

MODEL

The Book Thief is a nontraditional story in some ways. In the first glance at its pages, readers can see that it is not structured by standard-size paragraphs, with alternating description and dialogue, the way most works of fiction are. The structure seems free-form, as if the narrator is jotting down observations and comments as they occur to him. A close look, however, shows that *The Book Thief* contains all the tried and true elements of an enthralling narrative. The story begins as follows:

> First the **colors.**
> Then the **humans.**
> That's usually how **I** see things.
> Or at least, how I try.

Please note that excerpts and passages in the StudySync® library and this workbook are intended as touchstones to generate interest in an author's work. The excerpts and passages do not substitute for the reading of entire texts, and StudySync® strongly recommends that students seek out and purchase the whole literary or informational work in order to experience it as the author intended. Links to online resellers are available in our digital library. In addition, complete works may be ordered through an authorized reseller by filling out and returning to StudySync® the order form enclosed in this workbook.

Reading & Writing Companion

97

HERE IS A SMALL FACT

You are going to die

I am in all truthfulness **attempting to be cheerful** about **this whole topic . . .** Just don't ask me to be nice. **Nice has nothing to do with me.**

At this point, the reader might be wondering, "What kind of way is that to begin a story?" But this cryptic beginning provides a lot of information about character, theme, and plot. The reader can tell from the use of the word "I" that the narrator is first-person, and that the narrating character is a strange—though as yet, unnamed—individual who thinks about deep themes such as life and death, and who has a grim sense of humor and a friendly, but also oddly threatening, tone. The setting is not specifically described, but readers know it involves colors and humans. The reader's interest is aroused, and the reader expects that as the narrative continues, answers and identities will become clear. In fact, before long, it becomes fairly clear that the narrator is none other than Death himself:

> I could introduce myself properly, but it is not really necessary. You will know me well enough and soon enough, depending on a diverse range of variables. It suffices to say that at some point in time, I will be standing over you, as genially as possible. Your soul will be in my arms.

More of the setting and the exposition of the plot appears when the narrator begins to interact with other characters. The setting is given in the title of Part 2: "BESIDE THE RAILWAY LINE." The characters are described, and dialogue and details appear:

> Next to the **train line,** footprints were sunken to their shins. Trees wore blankets of ice.
>
> As you might expect, someone had died.
>
> They couldn't just leave him on the ground. For now, it wasn't such a problem, but very soon, the track ahead would be cleared and the train would need to move on.
>
> There were **two guards.**
>
> There was **one mother and her daughter.**
>
> **One corpse.**
>
> The mother, the girl, and the corpse remained stubborn and silent.
>
> "Well, what else do you want me to do?"

The guards were tall and short. **The tall one always spoke first, though he was not in charge.** He looked at the smaller, rounder one. The one with the juicy red face.

"Well," was the response, "we can't just leave them like this, can we?"

The tall one was losing patience. "Why not?"

In only a few words, the narrator has sketched a snowy scene by a railroad track, featuring a group of people who have specific roles with regard to each other. Two, a mother and daughter, are suffering. Two are guarding them, and the guard who is officially in charge seems weaker than the other guard. And there's a corpse. And that spooky narrator.

The dialogue is minimal, but nothing more needs to be said at this point. It is clear that terrible pain, and probably violence and injustice, are at play. The guards are unsure of how cruel or kind they are supposed to be. A corpse cannot interact, but the minds and imaginations of all the other characters are surely interacting with it in different ways. The narrator does not intervene—in fact, the other characters seem unaware of his presence—but dealing with death is a powerful kind of interaction, likely to reveal the truth about the characters.

In a short space, the author of *The Book Thief* has touched on all the important narrative elements—including narrator, setting, character, plot, and conflict— and likely made readers hungry for more.

 PRACTICE

Name your three favorite stories that involve an unusual interaction—either between two characters or between a character and some other force, such as nature or time. For each story, identify what conflict or problem the character or characters face in what kind of setting; what type of interaction takes place to create, develop, intensify, or help solve the conflict; and what narrative point of view the story employs. Describe any trends or patterns you notice in what kinds of characters, settings, conflicts, and interactions— and which type of narrator—you find most interesting or engaging as a reader. Doing so may help you identify the kind of story you want to tell. Exchange your work with a partner to give and receive feedback about your ideas.

NOTES

PREWRITE

CA-CCSS: CA.W.9-10.3a, CA.W.9-10.5, CA.W.9-10.6, CA.SL.9-10.1a, CA.SL.9-10.1b, CA.SL.9-10.1c, CA.SL.9-10.1d

WRITING PROMPT

Consider the unusual interactions presented in *The Book Thief* (Death and a survivor) as well as *An American Childhood* (a girl and her environment). Write a narrative about an unusual interaction that takes place between a character and someone or something else (such as another person, animal, object, entity, or environment) that reveals the character's true nature or affects the character in a meaningful way. The narrative may reflect real or imagined experiences or events.

Your narrative should include:

- an unusual interaction that reveals or affects the main character
- a plot—a sequence of connected events with a beginning, middle, and end that explores a conflict to be resolved
- a clear narrative point of view
- vividly described characters and realistic dialogue
- precise words and phrases that appeal to the senses
- a conclusion that effectively follows from and wraps up the narrative

For your extended writing project, you will use narrative writing techniques to compose a narrative in which interactions between characters—or between the main character and an outside force such as nature, death, or time—play a central role.

Writers often take notes about story ideas before they sit down to write. Some writers list ideas about characters, plot, and other elements, and then choose the ones they think will be most entertaining for readers—and for them as

writers. Others start with a beginning and an ending and then sketch out possibilities for events that could lead the characters through the plot.

Think about what you have learned so far about organizing narrative writing. What kinds of characters would you like to write about in your narrative? How would they interact? What kinds of conflict might the main character face? From which point of view should your story be told, and why?

Make a list of answers to these questions by completing the "Prewrite: Narrative Writing" chart. Record your brainstorming ideas about the characters and their interactions (with other characters or with forces or entities such as nature, time, or death), the conflict, and the narrator. Then look over your ideas and choose the details that create the story you want to write. Use the chart on the following page, completed by the writer of the Student Model narrative, to help guide your prewriting:

Copyright © BookheadEd Learning, LLC

NOTES

PREWRITE – NARRATIVE WRITING

Characters	Interaction	Conflict	Narrator
What characters would I like to write about?	*How might these characters interact in unusual or meaningful ways?*	*What conflict might the main character need to address?*	*From which point of view should this story be told? Why?*
A teen and parent	One helps the other overcome a problem.	Something bad has happened. He or she struggles to cope with it.	First person, from the main character's point of view, so readers can better relate to that person's feelings.
Two teenage friends	They have a huge argument.	He or she faces problems in a close relationship.	
A teen who is moving and someone he or she is leaving behind	One coaxes the other into trouble.		First person, from the other's character's point of view, so readers gain insight into how the main character is perceived by others.
A brother and sister	One discovers a secret about the other.	He or she doesn't know whether to tell the truth or keep silent about something.	
		He or she wants something that another isn't prepared to give.	Third person, so readers can view the events from an objective perspective and form our own impressions of both characters.

SKILL: INTRODUCTIONS

DEFINE

The **introduction** is the opening of the narrative; it sets the stage for the events to come. Because the introduction is the reader's first experience with the story, writers often include elements of **exposition**—essential information such as character, setting, and problem—in the opening paragraphs of the story. A story's introduction should capture the reader's attention and tempt him or her to move forward into the story with interest. After reading a paragraph or a few paragraphs, a reader should think, "I wonder what will happen. I'd like to keep reading and discover more about these characters." A good introduction hooks a reader with precise language and sensory details that bring the reader into the world of the story.

Identification and Application:

- A narrative introduction should provide the reader with a sense of the story's setting.

- The introduction usually signals the story's narrative point of view, such as through the narrator's use of personal pronouns.

- Writers often introduce main characters in the opening paragraphs of a story.

- A writer may present the story's main problem, or conflict, in the introductory paragraphs, to engage the reader with the events to come.

- The opening scene of a story may contain an action that sets a sequence of events—the plot—in motion.

- Writers make precise word choices, often infusing narrative introductions with vivid sensory details that draw readers into the story.

IDENTIFICATION AND APPLICATION

A skillful writer can lead the reader to imagine an entire world in the first few sentences of a story. Not all the details of that invented world and its people will be evident yet, but the reader will have been given clues. For example, here's the first paragraph of "Catch the Moon":

Luis Cintrón sits on top of a six-foot pile of hubcaps and watches **his father** walk away into the steel jungle of **his car junkyard. Released into his old man's custody after six** months in **juvenile hall**—for **breaking and entering**—and **he didn't even take anything. He did it on a dare.** But **the old lady with the million cats** was a light sleeper, and good with **her aluminum cane. He has a scar on his head** to prove it.

There's an amazing amount of introductory information there, as well as descriptive details about the character that practically dare the reader not to want to know more. So far, the reader knows that:

- The main character is a young man named Luis Cintrón, who was just released from juvenile hall after six months.
- Luis committed a crime by breaking and entering on a dare, but he didn't steal anything.
- An old lady, the owner of many cats, caught him in the act and hit him with her cane, injuring his scalp.
- Luis's sentence was longer than six months, but his father got him out early by giving him a job.
- The job is at a junkyard his father owns, which is the setting of the introductory scene.
- Luis doesn't like the junkyard, and is resentful about what's happened to him.
- The narration is third-person limited, meaning that the narrator is not Luis but reveals Luis's thoughts.

The list of things the reader knows is longer than the text that gives the information! And it doesn't even include descriptive details such as the six-foot pile of hubcaps Luis sits on.

The second paragraph of "Catch the Moon" can also be considered part of the introduction, because it continues providing exposition about the basic setup of the story:

Now Luis is wondering whether he should have stayed in and done his full time. Jorge Cintrón of Jorge Cintrón & Son, Auto Parts and Salvage, has decided that Luis should wash and polish every hubcap in the yard. The hill he is sitting on is only the latest couple of hundred wheel covers that have come in. Luis grunts and stands up on top of his silver mountain. He yells at no one, "Someday, son, all this will be yours," and sweeps his arms like the Pope blessing a crowd over the piles of car sandwiches and mounds of metal parts that cover this acre of land outside the city. He is the "Son" of Jorge Cintrón & Son, and so far his father has had more than one reason to wish it was plain Jorge Cintrón on the sign.

 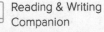

A list of things the reader learns from that paragraph could probably go on for half a page. It adds new expository information and many details. It describes the setting of the junkyard more vividly. It clarifies that Luis's father strongly wants him to work at the junkyard and, someday, take over the business—but that Luis doesn't necessarily share his dream. It lets the reader know that the third-person-limited narrator is likely to continue showing Luis's thoughts and feelings, and not his father's.

There has been little action so far, and that's often the case with the introduction, or exposition, of a story. The important thing is that it makes the reader eager to find out what will happen next to these people.

 ## PRACTICE

Write an introduction for your narrative that establishes the main character, the narrative point of view, and the setting. When you are finished, trade with a partner and offer each other feedback. How precise is the language used in your partner's introduction? How well do the details help you to picture the setting and characters? What do you learn about the main character, and possibly other characters, from the introduction? What questions does the introduction raise with you that you hope the rest of the story will answer? Offer each other suggestions, and remember that they are most helpful when they are constructive.

SKILL: NARRATIVE TECHNIQUES AND SEQUENCING

⭐ DEFINE

To write a story, writers use a variety of tools to develop the plot and characters, explore the setting, and engage the reader. **Narrative techniques** include dialogue, pacing, description, reflection, and the sequencing of events, which may sometimes include multiple plot lines. **Dialogue,** what the characters say to one another, is often used to develop characters and forward the action of the plot. Writers often manipulate the **pacing** of a narrative, or the speed with which events occur, to slow down or speed up the action at certain points of a story. Writers use **description** to build story details and reveal information about character, setting, and plot. Narrators and characters often engage in **reflection,** pondering the events that have occurred so far in the story. Every narrative contains a **sequence of events**, which is carefully planned and controlled by the author as the story unfolds. Longer narratives, such as novels, often contain **multiple plot lines** consisting of a main plot and one or more **subplots,** which may be connected through their characters, events, and themes.

The sequence of events in a story builds a **plot**—a chain or web or organized, related events that are introduced at the beginning, or **exposition,** gather momentum through the middle—the **rising action** and the **climax**—and come to a conclusion in the **falling action** and the **resolution**. The sequence of events in a narrative may proceed in a straight chronological line from the first event that occurs to the last event that occurs. In many cases, however, authors build detours in the sequence, most often by inserting **flashbacks.** A flashback is a scene that returns to an earlier event in the sequence. It may have taken place before the main plot sequence began. Usually, flashbacks fill in background information that helps readers understand the events of the main sequence.

The ultimate purpose of all these narrative techniques is similar: to keep readers reading.

IDENTIFICATION AND APPLICATION

- A narrative outline can help writers organize a sequence of events before they begin writing a story.
- A narrative outline should follow this framework:
  › exposition, rising action (conflict), climax, falling action, resolution
  › The sequence may be narrated strictly from first event to last event or may include scenes out of sequence, such as flashbacks.

- The exposition contains essential information for the reader, such as characters, setting, and the problem or conflict the characters will face.
  › Settings are shown in descriptions and can influence events.
  › Writers often include details to reveal the elements of the exposition without directly stating these elements for the reader.
  › Readers should feel interested during the exposition and wonder, "What will happen in this story?"

- In the rising action, a writer begins to develop plot and character.
  › Characters are developed through dialogue, action, and description.
  › The rising action introduces and builds on the conflict until the story reaches the climax.
  › During the rising action, readers should feel invested in the story and care about what is going to happen next.

- The climax is the turning point in the story, often where the most exciting action takes place.
  › Pacing is a technique writers use to control the speed of the way events are revealed. For example, reflection slows down the forward motion of the story and gives writers a chance to further develop the characters and plot.
  › The events that take place during the climax often force characters into action.
  › Readers should feel tense or excited during the climax and wonder, "How will the characters move forward?"

- The details and events that follow the climax make up the falling action of the story.
  › The events that take place during the climax should lead to the resolution.
  › During the falling action, readers should feel anxious to know how the story will end and wonder, "How will the conflict be resolved?"

Please note that excerpts and passages in the StudySync® library and this workbook are intended as touchstones to generate interest in an author's work. The excerpts and passages do not substitute for the reading of entire texts, and StudySync® strongly recommends that students seek out and purchase the whole literary or informational work in order to experience it as the author intended. Links to online resellers are available in our digital library. In addition, complete works may be ordered through an authorized reseller by filling out and returning to StudySync® the order form enclosed in this workbook.

Reading & Writing Companion   **107**

- The story must end in resolution of the conflict.
  › The way the problem has developed and moves toward resolution should be logical and feel natural to the story.
  › The resolution should explain—with no room for doubt—how the characters resolved the conflict.
  › By the end of the story, readers should feel satisfied and entertained and think, "That was a great story!"

MODEL

In the story "Kelsey and the Poet," the student writer uses narrative techniques and sequencing to develop events and characters. Let's examine this excerpt:

Sharif read Kelsey's poem over her shoulder. "May I? 'First Feelings.' I like that title. How old are you?"

"Fifteen, and this is the first manuscript I've ever sent anywhere, and I'm already a miserable failure! This is a terrible omen! I'm never going to do anything worthwhile! I'm doomed for life!"

Kelsey remembered how excited she'd been when she first mailed the poem to the magazine. **She'd been positive that all she had to do was wait a couple of weeks** and there'd be an answering letter—no, a thrilled, thrilling phone call—telling her that the magazine was honored to have discovered America's newest literary talent. **She'd bought herself an ice cream sundae just to celebrate mailing the stupid thing!**

Being fifteen is a total embarrassment, Kelsey thought, especially when you're not a published poet yet. She gritted her teeth at the futility of her efforts.

"I think I was seventeen when I got my first rejection," Sharif said understandingly. "I had a similar attitude, if I remember correctly."

She gave him a look of surprise. "Are you a poet too?"

"I sure am." Without warning he poured forth words about someone taking a long walk, who was the speaker of the poem. **They were beautiful, sorrowful, silken, somehow violet-colored words about not knowing what to do.** They might have been written just for her.

In this exchange of dialogue, the author presents readers with many details that fill in the outlines of the two characters. Most obviously, the dialogue—the conversation between Kelsey and Sharif—helps the reader see, hear, and understand the characters in detail. Their style of speech is natural, believable, and subtly different from each other: Basically, Kelsey talks like an enthusiastic, excitable teen and Sharif talks like a sympathetic, understanding adult who probably remembers when he was more excitable himself. In addition, basic plot information is conveyed in this dialogue—namely, that Kelsey had sent a poem to a magazine and that she has just received a rejection letter. The dialogue provides the medium for the exchange between the two characters, and in this story, the events consist largely of character interaction.

Other narrative techniques in this passage bring it further to life. When Sharif reads his poem aloud, descriptions help the reader feel the impact of the words on Kelsey through vivid description: "They were beautiful, sorrowful, silken, somehow violet-colored words about not knowing what to do." Without even knowing the exact words of Sharif's poem, the reader of the story gets a sense of what they mean and even how they sound.

The most basic purpose of description in narrative is to make the reader see, hear, and feel the experiences of the story. The description of Sharif reading also has another technical purpose: it slows down the pace of the scene at a crucial point. The dialogue sections of the scene tend to be fast; Kelsey and Sharif exchange lines of banter back and forth without pausing. Sharif's reading of the poem creates a pause in the dialogue, and since the words of the poem aren't included in the dialogue, the pause is even clearer, because it's conveyed entirely in description, which takes longer to read than dialogue. This change of pace is rewarding for its own sake—who doesn't like a change now and then?—and it also makes this part of the scene feel more thoughtful or more, well, *poetic*.

Reflection also occurs when Kelsey ponders her own actions and traits: "Being fifteen is a total embarrassment, Kelsey thought, especially when you're not a published poet yet." These lines slow the narrative pace but also reveal Kelsey's character: she is dramatic and naive, but also thoughtful, self-aware, and ambitious.

In this story, reflection goes hand in hand with a shift in the sequence of events—a flashback because the flashback is in the form of a memory of Kelsey's. The clause, "Kelsey remembered how excited she'd been" tells the reader that Kelsey is looking back into her past. The writer uses the phrases "she'd been" and "she'd bought" instead of "she was" and "she bought," thus employing grammar to signal a shift in the sequence of events.

It's important to note that narrative techniques don't always occur in isolation. More than one technique can be at work in the same sentence, or even the same phrase or word. For example, descriptions of actions, people, and places can often be found within characters' words of dialogue. A writer's job is to juggle all of the narrative elements to create a compelling story.

By juggling narrative techniques effectively, the writer of the Student Model has crafted an engaging interaction that points the story toward its climax. A outline of the story's rising action might look as follows:

I. Rising Action
    A. Kelsey reacts dramatically to the magazine's rejection of her poems.
    B. Kelsey flashes back to when she mailed the poems, recalling with disappointment and humiliation how excited she'd been.
    C. Kelsey reflects on how being fifteen is "a total embarrassment."
    D. Sharif sympathizes by telling Kelsey that he got his first rejection when he was about her age and felt the same way.
    E. Kelsey expresses surprise that Sharif, a mail carrier, is also a poet.
    F. Sharif shares "somehow violet-colored words" from a poem he's written; to Kelsey, they "might have been written just for her."

 PRACTICE

Create an outline of the sequence of events that might make up the rising action in your narrative about an interaction. As you create your outline, consider the characters, conflict, setting, interaction, and narrative point of view you identified in the Prewrite stage and the exposition you began to develop in your introduction. What events will follow this introduction and form your story's rising action? How might you use dialogue and pacing to propel the action and advance the plot in this part of the narrative? How might reflection on the part of the main character or manipulating time, such as through a flashback, enhance the narrative? When you are finished, exchange outlines with a partner to offer and receive feedback.

CA-CCSS: CA.W.9-10.3a, CA.W.9-10.3b, CA.W.9-10.3c, CA.W.9-10.5, CA.W.9-10.10, CA.SL.9-10.1c

PLAN

NOTES

WRITING PROMPT

Consider the unusual interactions presented in *The Book Thief* (Death and a survivor) as well as *An American Childhood* (a girl and her environment). Write a narrative about an unusual interaction that takes place between a character and someone or something else (such as another person, animal, object, entity, or environment) that reveals the character's true nature or affects the character in a meaningful way. The narrative may reflect real or imagined experiences or events.

Your narrative should include:

- an unusual interaction that reveals or affects the main character
- a plot—a sequence of connected events with a beginning, middle, and end that explores a conflict to be resolved
- a clear narrative point of view
- vividly described characters and realistic dialogue
- precise words and phrases that appeal to the senses
- a conclusion that effectively follows from and wraps up the narrative

Think about the elements of narrative that you studied in the Narrative Techniques and Sequencing lesson. Ask yourself the following questions to solidify your understanding:

- What details and events are most important in the exposition of a story?
- What story developments should take place during the rising action of a story?
- What is the purpose of a story's climax?
- How do writers lead readers toward a resolution of a story?

- What makes for a satisfying resolution?
- What narrative techniques are the most effective?

Use the *Narrative Plot Diagram* to plan a sequence of events for your narrative. Use this plot diagram, completed by the writer of the Student Model, to help guide your planning:

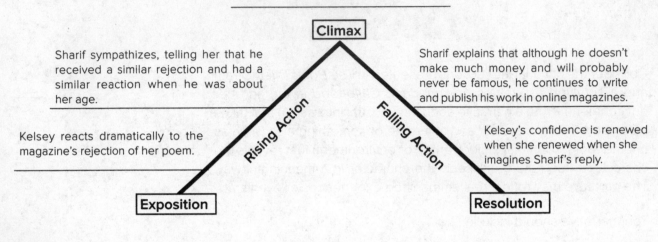

Sharif explains that he too is a poet and shares his "violet-colored" words, which Kelsey feels are "written for her."

Climax

Sharif sympathizes, telling her that he received a similar rejection and had a similar reaction when he was about her age.

Sharif explains that although he doesn't make much money and will probably never be famous, he continues to write and publish his work in online magazines.

Rising Action

Falling Action

Kelsey reacts dramatically to the magazine's rejection of her poem.

Kelsey's confidence is renewed when she renewed when she imagines Sharif's reply.

Exposition

Resolution

SKILL:
WRITING
DIALOGUE

 DEFINE

Dialogue Is one of the primary tools of narrative writing. Dialogue is speech between two or more characters. Dialogue is the heart of many interactions between characters, and it can also provide details in place of a descriptive narrative by illuminating a character's personality, advancing the plot, revealing details that lend insight to the driving conflict, or showcasing the setting of a narrative by using regionally or historically specific vernacular.

There are two different types of dialogue: direct and indirect. **Direct dialogue** is speech that uses a character's exact words. Direct dialogue is placed between quotation marks. Direct dialogue is the kind that is most commonly found in fiction. An example of direct dialogue would be:

"Please remember to do the laundry," Elena said.

Indirect dialogue is a second-hand report of something that was said or written, without quoting the character's exact words. Quotation marks are not used for indirect dialogue. An example of indirect dialogue would be:

Elena asked Ron to do the laundry, and Ron assured her that he would.

In dialogue between characters, it should always be clear who is speaking which lines. Speech tags such as s*he said, he replied, she demanded,* and *he shouted* identify the speakers and, sometimes, their tone of voice. If the identity of the speaker is completely clear, such as if two characters have been exchanging one line at a time during a long conversation, then speech tags are sometimes omitted. Correct punctuation is important when writing dialogue.

NOTES

IDENTIFICATION AND APPLICATION

Though every writer's style can differ, there are a few basic guidelines to follow when using **direct dialogue** in your narrative:

- Use open (") and closed (") quotation marks to indicate the words that are spoken by the characters.
- Always begin a new paragraph when the speaker changes.
- Make sure the reader knows who is saying what.
- When writing an interaction between characters, the author can use phrases other than simply "he said", "she said", or "they said." Depending on the nature or emotion of character's quotation, it can be accompanied by stronger verbs, adjective phrases, or adverbs. However, when in doubt, "said" and "asked" are the most reliable choices.
- Use correct punctuation marks and capitalization.

Use **indirect dialogue** without quotation marks

- when the exact words spoken are not important enough to the narrative to be showcased, but the occurrence and details of the conversation are important for the reader to know.
- when a character is describing or paraphrasing an interaction he or she had.

Writers can use both direct and indirect dialogue to develop characters by revealing the characters' opinions, reactions, emotions, experiences, personalities, and even appearances through

- what the characters say (direct or indirect speech).
- how the characters say it (their speech patterns; the vocabulary and level of language they use).
- the way the characters say it (usually following the quote; such as *said happily* or *yelled angrily*).
- the characters' body language as they are speaking (such as *said, smiling*).
- the characters' actions as they are speaking (such as *responded, twirling a lock of her hair*).
- the characters' thoughts as they are speaking (such as *"I'd rather not go there," he said, reflecting that he'd absolutely refuse to go there under any circumstances*).

MODEL

Read the following passage of dialogue from "Kelsey and the Poet" to see how the author uses direct dialogue:

> "Oh, no!" she cried out.
>
> "They sent it back," Sharif said, understandingly.
>
> "This is terrible. I'll never get anything published."
>
> Sharif read Kelsey's poem over her shoulder. "May I? 'First Feelings.' I like that title. How old are you?"
>
> "Fifteen, and this is the first manuscript I've ever sent anywhere, and I'm already a miserable failure! This is a terrible omen! I'm never going to do anything worthwhile! I'm doomed for life!"

In this conversation, Kelsey and Sharif tell each other a good deal of information about themselves—which means that they tell the reader, too. In addition, their way of speaking helps characterize them. For instance, Kelsey's overwrought emotional exclamations show that she is a sensitive teenager, and her vocabulary shows her intelligence.

This excerpt also shows that the writer has followed the technical guidelines for direct dialogue. She has set off the direct speech of each character with open quotation marks. She also

- places the closed quotation marks outside the end punctuation of the quote, while the rest of the sentence has its own end punctuation.
- begins a new paragraph when the speaker changes.
- makes sure the reader knows who is saying what ("she cried out," "Sharif said understandingly").

Now let's look at a second excerpt to see how the writer uses indirect dialogue:

> He laughed again, and told her that no, he probably never would be, except among a couple of hundred people—but, he added, they were people who really understood poetry.

Within this passage, the writer uses indirect dialogue to give the reader more information about Sharif, through the process of Sharif providing Kelsey with

Please note that excerpts and passages in the StudySync® library and this workbook are intended as touchstones to generate interest in an author's work. The excerpts and passages do not substitute for the reading of entire texts, and StudySync® strongly recommends that students seek out and purchase the whole literary or informational work in order to experience it as the author intended. Links to online resellers are available in our digital library. In addition, complete works may be ordered through an authorized reseller by filling out and returning to StudySync® the order form enclosed in this workbook.

Reading & Writing Companion   **115**

NOTES

that information. Although the writer could have invented direct dialogue for the same purpose, she decided that indirect dialogue works better in this particular passage. It makes Sharif's response "sound" quieter and more thoughtful; this way, it's easier for the reader to tell that the prospect of never becoming well-known makes him sad but also resigned. The use of indirect dialogue in the passage above creates a subtle change of mood, making it somewhat subdued compared to the direct dialogue. At the same time, the description, "He laughed again," implies that Sharif has made his peace with the realities of life.

In short, indirect dialogue can help enhance the process of characterization as well as convey important information about events. Although not apparent in this excerpt, indirect dialogue can also be an exciting technique if

- a character interprets another character's intent or emotions, putting a "spin" on what he or she said.
- we as readers witness the original conversation, and then, through a character's paraphrasing of the conversation, discover that the character is lying about it to serve his or her own purpose.

Through the use of dialogue in "Kelsey and the Poet," we as readers learn not only about the subject being discussed, but who the characters are: how they sound, how they feel, how they interact with people, and a considerable amount about their lives. Dialogue performs many jobs within a narrative—sometimes, several jobs at once.

 ## PRACTICE

Write a passage for your narrative in which two or more characters engage in both direct and indirect dialogue. When you are finished, trade with a partner and offer each other feedback. Has the writer followed the technical guidelines for direct dialogue? Do you see areas where the indirect dialogue can be improved? How does the dialogue help develop character? Does the dialogue reveal information about the plot? Offer each other suggestions, and remember that they are most helpful when they are constructive.

SKILL: CONCLUSIONS

⭐ DEFINE

A narrative **conclusion** is the story's end. It reflects on what has occurred during the narrative—what the characters have experienced and observed, what problems they have faced, and in what state they now find themselves after the **resolution** (or lack thereof) of these problems. In **fiction** narratives, the conclusion brings the **plot** to an end: the main **conflict** has been dealt with, the **climax** has been lived through, and a resolution has been arrived at. In **nonfiction** narratives, such as **memoir,** the conclusion often represents the opening of a new stage of life or a new understanding on the part of the author. The conclusion may point toward or hint at the characters' future without actually describing it, for the future is another story, which the writer may or may not ever write. At the conclusion, the main character might **reflect** on what has occurred and on the changes that have occurred within him or her. Or a different character might reflect based on observations of the main character. Or a **third-person narrator** might reflect on the events or give hints about what impact they have had. In most stories, the main character has been **transformed,** or changed, in a significant way. The conclusion is the place where such a transformation is most strongly revealed or suggested to the reader. After the **falling action,** the resolution settles the situation down into a calmer state, allowing the reader to form a lasting impression of the people, events, and **themes.** The author's hope is that the reader will carry that impression around for a long time after closing the story's final pages.

••• IDENTIFICATION AND APPLICATION

- A narrative conclusion includes the final actions and events in the story.
- Especially in fiction and often in nonfiction narratives, the conclusion presents a resolution of the conflict that the main character faced.
- Conclusions often focus on a final interaction between characters who have faced the main problem in the narrative.

- Authors often use descriptive details to elicit an emotional response from the reader upon a narrative's conclusion.
- A narrative conclusion often conveys the author's theme, or central idea, either through explicit statements or through a scene that allows the reader to infer the theme.
- The conclusion is the natural place for a final reflection by the narrator or main character, such as on the characters' lives and transformations and on the ideas the story has developed.
- A strong narrative conclusion leaves the reader with a lasting impression of the narrative that enhances the reader's memory of the work.

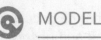 MODEL

In Annie Dillard's memoir *An American Childhood*, the author describes what it looked and felt like to be a child growing up in the 1950s United States in the aftermath of World War II. Dillard's poetic, sensitive observations run throughout the memoir, but in this excerpt, the conclusion brings them to a fine point of greater understanding—not only about the author's childhood, but about what it means to be alive, to be a person who observes and thinks and feels.

A text does not usually come with a note saying "The conclusion begins here," but in this excerpt the sentence beginning, "What a marvel it was," signals that the narrator is turning from descriptions of specific scenes to more general reflections:

> **What a marvel it was** that the day so often introduced itself with a firm footfall nearby. What a marvel it was that so many times a day the world, like a church bell, reminded me **to recall and contemplate the durable fact that I was here,** and had awakened once more **to find myself set down in a going world.**

This paragraph is not just about the sounds and events on the street where Dillard grew up. It is about the whole world. Most conclusions do not get that deep! But it is an example of how conclusions can move from the specifics of a storyline to larger concerns—to what Dillard calls "the sum of those moments" that have gone before. And that is realistic, because our experiences do sometimes cause us to think beyond what has immediately happened.

Dillard's conclusion returns to specific description in the next paragraph, but the final two paragraphs are pure reflection:

NOTES

Who could ever tire of this heart-stopping transition, of **this breakthrough shift between seeing and knowing you see, between being and knowing you be? It drives you to a life of concentration,** it does, a life in which effort draws you down so very deep that when you surface you twist up exhilarated with a yelp and a gasp.

Who could ever tire of **this radiant transition, this surfacing to awareness** and this deliberate plunging to oblivion—the theater curtain rising and falling? Who could tire of it when **the sum of those moments** at the edge—the conscious life we so dread losing—is all we have, the gift at the moment of opening it?

In addition to presenting a profound observation, this passage strengthens the characterization of the author/main character, Annie Dillard, as someone with a vast imagination and highly individual thought processes, certainly as an adult and even to some extent as a child. The passage resolves the character's emotional conflict about her existence. She asks, "Am I living?" and receives a resounding affirmative from her environment. It also expresses the adult writer's reflection upon the deep significance of those intense, solitary moments as a child. This conclusion also gives further proof of what the reader has noticed all along—that Dillard is a very fine stylist in prose, really a kind of prose poet, who consistently devises unpredictable figurative comparisons ("the world, like a church bell"), original descriptive wordings ("you twist up exhilarated"), even distortions of grammar ("between being and knowing you be") to convey profound insights about the experience of being alive.

This conclusion leaves a lasting impression.

 ## PRACTICE

Plan and draft a conclusion to the narrative you have been prewriting and planning for this unit's extended writing assignment. Consider what you have learned from this lesson about how to use your conclusion to wrap up the plot and the characters' conflicts or interactions. Try to make your conclusion insightful and memorable. Practice using strong verbs, concrete nouns, and varied, interesting sentence structures. When you are finished, trade with a partner and offer each other feedback. Does this conclusion draft give you confidence that the writer's story will have an effective ending with a decisive resolution? Does the narrative leave you with a lasting impression, perhaps through an intriguing or insightful final thought? What do you wish this conclusion had more of, or less of? Offer suggestions, and remember that they are most helpful when they are constructive.

DRAFT

CA-CCSS: CA.W.9-10.3a, CA.W.9-10.3b, CA.W.9-10.3c, CA.W.9-10.3d, CA.W.9-10.3e, CA.W.9-10.4, CA.W.9-10.5, CA.W.9-10.6, CA.W.9-10.10, CA.SL.9-10.1a, CA.L.9-10.1b, CA.L.9-10.1c, CA.L.9-10.6

WRITING PROMPT

Consider the unusual interactions presented in *The Book Thief* (Death and a survivor) as well as *An American Childhood* (a girl and her environment). Write a narrative about an unusual interaction that takes place between a character and someone or something else (such as another person, animal, object, entity, or environment) that reveals the character's true nature or affects the character in a meaningful way. The narrative may reflect real or imagined experiences or events.

Your narrative should include:

- an unusual interaction that reveals or affects the main character
- a plot—a sequence of connected events with a beginning, middle, and end that explores a conflict to be resolved
- a clear narrative point of view
- vividly described characters and realistic dialogue
- precise words and phrases that appeal to the senses
- a conclusion that effectively follows from and wraps up the narrative

You have already made progress toward writing your narrative. You have planned your story and thought about how writers use event sequences, point of view, dialogue, descriptive details, and pacing to bring a narrative to life. You have drafted your introductory paragraphs and a passage containing dialogue, and you have practiced writing a strong and effective conclusion. You have also considered how your story would connect with its audience and serve its intended purpose. Now it is time to write a full draft of your narrative.

Use your prewriting graphic organizer, plot diagram, practice drafts, and other prewriting materials to help you as you write. Remember that the in the rising action of a narrative, writers introduce characters, setting, and conflict and begin to develop characters and plot. The rising action leads to the story's climax, the turning point in the story, where the most exciting action takes place. The falling action of a story occurs after the climax and leads to the resolution of the conflict and the story's conclusion. Keep readers in mind as you write, and aim to keep your audience interested.

When drafting, ask yourself these questions:

- What would be the most interesting and effective narrative point of view for this particular story?
- What can I do to improve my introduction so that readers understand expository information early in my story?
- What can I do to clarify and strengthen the sequence of events?
- How can I use dialogue to reveal character and advance the plot?
- How can I use pacing to make my story an engaging reading experience?
- What details can I improve and expand on to make events, characters, and settings clearer and more vivid?
- How will I resolve the story's conflict in a way that is satisfying and memorable?
- Have I used noun clauses effectively?

Before you submit your draft, read it over carefully. You want to be sure that you have responded to all aspects of the prompt.

NOTES

SKILL:
TRANSITIONS

⭐ DEFINE

Transitions clarify the relationship of words and ideas. The use of transition words, clauses, and phrases helps readers understand and follow the structure of a narrative. Writers use time-order words and phrases and clauses (for example, *first, the following day,* and *soon after*) to transition from one event to the next. Transitions can also signal a change in the setting, or where a story takes place. Spatial transitions such as *on top of, behind, near,* and *to the left* help describe the settings of actions and the spatial relationships of objects or people. Transitional phrases such as *but, in addition, on the other hand,* and *as a result,* when they appear at the beginning of a paragraph, show how ideas are related to those in the previous paragraph.

••• IDENTIFICATION AND APPLICATION

- Transitions act like bridges between sentences or paragraphs.
- Narrative writers use transitions to signal shifts in time or setting.
- Transitions help writers to convey the sequence of events in a story.
- Writers can also use transitions to show the relationships among character experiences and story events.

◎ MODEL

This excerpt from *The Book Thief* contains transitions that help the reader understand the setting and sequence of events. Let's read the passage to identify the transitions the author used:

> As for me, I had **already** made the most elementary of mistakes. I can't explain to you the severity of my self-disappointment. **Originally,** I'd done everything right.

NOTES

I studied the blinding, white-snow sky who stood at the window of the moving train. I practically inhaled it, **but still,** I wavered. I buckled—I became interested. In the girl. Curiosity got the better of me, and I resigned myself to stay as long as my schedule allowed, and I watched.

Twenty-three minutes later, when the train was stopped, I climbed **out** with them. A small soul was in my arms.

I stood a little **to the right.**

In the first paragraph from this excerpt, the narrator uses the **time word** "already" as a **transition** to show that he is about to say something about what happened previously. This transition word indicates a change in the narrative sequence—a brief **flashback.** The word "originally," in the same paragraph, also serves as a transition showing that the narrator is casting a glance backward in time, at something that had happened earlier. Two paragraphs later, the phrase "Twenty-three minutes later" is a transition that moves the action forward in time. In fact, with that phrase, the sequence of events has jumped forward into the next scene, in which the train stops and the characters climb out. The narrator does not communicate anything about what happens during those twenty-three minutes. The transition enables the story to advance without going into unnecessary specifics and reinforces the idea that Death is doing something very out of the ordinary by remaining with a particular group of humans for so long.

The word "out" in "I climbed out with them" is a **spatial transition** that helps the reader visualize how the characters move from the setting of the train to the next setting, the platform. Another spatial transition is "to the right," which places the narrator physically in a specific spot.

There is also **a transition between ideas** in the passage: "but still." That phrase presents a **contrast** between the idea that comes before it and the idea that comes after it. The narrator "practically inhaled" the sky—he was enthralled by the scenery—but then his interest wavered and focused on the girl, something he regretted.

Whether they are about time, place, or ideas, transitions are **signals** that help the reader keep track of the narrative.

⚡ PRACTICE

Write one body paragraph for your narrative that uses transition words, clauses, and/or phrases. When you are finished, trade with a partner and offer each other feedback. How effective are the transitions in indicating the passage of time? How well do the transitions show relationships among character interactions, story events, and ideas? Offer each other constructive, respectful suggestions for revision.

REVISE

CA-CCSS: CA.W.9-10.3a, CA.W.9-10.3b, CA.W.9-10.3c, CA.W.9-10.3d, CA.W.9-10.3e, CA.W.9-10.4, CA.W.9-10.5, CA.W.9-10.6, CA.W.9-10.10, CA.SL.9-10.1c, CA.L.9-10.3a

WRITING PROMPT

Consider the unusual interactions presented in *The Book Thief* (Death and a survivor) as well as *An American Childhood* (a girl and her environment). Write a narrative about an unusual interaction that takes place between a character and someone or something else (such as another person, animal, object, entity, or environment) that reveals the character's true nature or affects the character in a meaningful way. The narrative may reflect real or imagined experiences or events.

Your narrative should include:

- an unusual interaction that reveals or affects the main character
- a plot—a sequence of connected events with a beginning, middle, and end that explores a conflict to be resolved
- a clear narrative point of view
- vividly described characters and realistic dialogue
- precise words and phrases that appeal to the senses
- a conclusion that effectively follows from and wraps up the narrative

You have written a draft of your narrative and received feedback from your classmates about how to improve it. Now you will revise your draft.

Here are some recommendations to help you revise:

- Review the suggestions made by your peers.
- Examine the introduction of your narrative.
  - › Do your introductory paragraphs contain expository information about your characters and setting?

> › Does your story's introduction help the reader identify and visualize the setting?
> › Have you introduced the conflict in the introductory paragraphs of your narrative?
> › Does your introduction contain details that will interest readers?

- Evaluate the sequencing of events in your narrative.
  > › Do the events in your narrative follow a logical order?
  > › Have you used transition words to signal shifts in time or setting?
  > › Does the sequence of events help build and develop the plot, including the main conflict?
  > › Does the sequence of events focus on interactions between the main character and other people, ideas, or forces?

- Examine the prose you have used to tell your story.
  > › Have you included descriptive details that help readers visualize the characters, setting, and events?
  > › Are your descriptive words and phrases precise, vivid, concrete, and clear?
  > › Do your transitions show the relationships among character experiences and story events?

- Look at the dialogue in your story.
  > › Do your characters address one another in direct dialogue?
  > › Does the dialogue reveal the characters' traits?
  > › Does the dialogue help build the conflict and advance the plot?
  > › Have you followed the technical guidelines for writing direct and indirect dialogue?
  > › Is it clear to readers who is speaking during dialogue passages?

- Evaluate the conclusion of your story.
  > › Does the conclusion present a satisfying, sensible resolution of the conflict?
  > › Have you crafted a conclusion that will leave the reader with a lasting impression of your story?
  > › Will your conclusion trigger an emotional response in readers?

- Check for and correct any instances of misplaced or dangling modifiers.

Use these questions to help you evaluate your narrative to determine areas that should be strengthened or improved. Then revise those areas.

EDIT, PROOFREAD, AND PUBLISH

CA-CCSS: CA.W.9-10.3a, CA.W.9-10.3b, CA.W.9-10.3c, CA.W.9-10.3d, CA.W.9-10.3e, CA.W.9-10.4, CA.W.9-10.5, CA.W.9-10.6, CA.W.9-10.10, CA.SL.9-10.1a, CA.SL.9-10.1b, CA.SL.9-10.1c, CA.SL.9-10.1d, CA.SL.9-10.4, CA.SL.9-10.6, CA.L.9-10.1b, CA.L.9-10.2c, CA.L.9-10.3a

WRITING PROMPT

Consider the unusual interactions presented in *The Book Thief* (Death and a survivor) as well as *An American Childhood* (a girl and her environment). Write a narrative about an unusual interaction that takes place between a character and someone or something else (such as another person, animal, object, entity, or environment) that reveals the character's true nature or affects the character in a meaningful way. The narrative may reflect real or imagined experiences or events.

Your narrative should include:

- an unusual interaction that reveals or affects the main character
- a plot—a sequence of connected events with a beginning, middle, and end that explores a conflict to be resolved
- a clear narrative point of view
- vividly described characters and realistic dialogue
- precise words and phrases that appeal to the senses
- a conclusion that effectively follows from and wraps up the narrative

You have revised your story and received input from your peers on that revision. Now it is time to edit and proofread your work to produce a final version. This is also your last chance to correct details before submitting your narrative. Have you included all the valuable suggestions from your peers? Ask yourself:

- Is the entire sequence of events in my plot logical, clear, and fully developed?

- Have I included precise details described in vivid, concrete language? Are there any last-minute word changes that I can make to help the reader better "see" and "hear" the characters and events?
- Does each character's dialogue sound realistic and serve to develop his or her personality?
- What more can I do to make my story more engaging to readers?

When you are satisfied with your work, move on to proofread it for errors.

- Have you formatted and punctuated dialogue correctly?
- Have you spelled all words correctly, particularly those with noun suffixes?
- Have you used noun clauses correctly?
- Have you avoided misplaced and dangling modifiers?
- Do your sentences and paragraphs flow smoothly?

Once you have made all your corrections and given your story a title, you are ready to submit and publish your work. You can distribute your writing to family and friends, post it on your blog, or submit it to a literary magazine or contest.

studysync®
Powered by BookheadEd Learning,LLC

Text Fulfillment Through StudySync

If you are interested in specific titles, please fill out the form below and we will check availability through our partners.

ORDER DETAILS

Date:

TITLE	AUTHOR	Paperback/ Hardcover	Specific Edition *If Applicable*	Quantity

SHIPPING INFORMATION

Contact:

Title:

School/District:

Address Line 1:

Address Line 2:

Zip or Postal Code:

Phone:

Mobile:

Email:

BILLING INFORMATION   ☐ SAME AS SHIPPING

Contact:

Title:

School/District:

Address Line 1:

Address Line 2:

Zip or Postal Code:

Phone:

Mobile:

Email:

PAYMENT INFORMATION

☐ CREDIT CARD

Name on Card:

Card Number:

Expiration Date:

Security Code:

☐ PO

Purchase Order Number:

StudySync Text Fulfillment, BookheadEd Learning, LLC
610 Daniel Young Drive | Sonoma, CA 95476